THE SURVIVOR'S GUIDE
TO CHURCH LIFE

The survivor's guide to church life

*How to handle
relationships
disagreements
disillusion
change*

James and Nina Rye

Inter-Varsity Press

INTER-VARSITY PRESS
38 De Montfort Street, Leicester LE1 7GP, UK.

Unless otherwise stated, Scripture quotations in this publication are from the Holy Bible, New International Version. Copyright © 1973, 1978, 1984 International Bible Society. Published in Great Britain by Hodder and Stoughton Ltd.

The song reproduced on p. 150 is 'Soften my Heart' by Graham Kendrick, © 1988 Make Way Music, PO Box 683, Hailsham, East Sussex BN27 4ZB, UK. All rights reserved. International copyright secured. Used by permission.

First published 1992

British Library Cataloguing in Publication Data

A catalogue record for this book is available from the British Library.

ISBN 0–85110–870–9

Set in Linotron Ehrhardt
Photoset by Parker Typesetting Service, Leicester
Printed in Great Britain by
Cox & Wyman Ltd, Reading, Berkshire

Inter-Varsity Press is the book-publishing division of the Universities and Colleges Christian Fellowship (formerly the Inter-Varsity Fellowship), a student movement linking Christian Unions in universities and colleges throughout the United Kingdom and the Republic of Ireland, and a member movement of the International Fellowship of Evangelical Students. For information about local and national activities write to UCCF, 38 De Montfort Street, Leicester LE1 7GP.

CONTENTS

FOREWORD

'Jesus I like; it's the church I just can't stand.' If I had £5 for every time I have heard these words from a non-Christian, I would soon be a wealthy man.

'We are moving on in God, but our church (or fellowship) keeps on resisting what the Lord wants to achieve among his people.' This comment from Christians could, again, offer me the prospect of considerable financial profit.

Such is the current perspective of so many people. Remarks like these, repeated so often, indicate a serious problem. Most of us find it far easier to enter into an individual relationship with Jesus Christ than to contemplate the implications of being part of his forever family.

The fact of the matter is that the Christian life was never intended to be a solo experience. A man once rode up to John Wesley and announced, 'Sir, if you want to serve God and get to heaven, you can never go there alone, for the Bible knows nothing of solitary religion.' Coming to Christ involves joining his people and discovering that we inherit numerous 'brothers and sisters'. We might not have chosen them, but we are lumbered with them!

In more sober moments, we do well to recognize that God has not only given us his Holy Spirit, he has also provided us with one another. This is 'church', not a building or an institutional structure, but friends and partners to encourage and support us in our service for Christ.

So why does 'church' so often fail to live up to our expectations? Does the fault lie with us, with the leadership, or with everyone else?

Many of us have suffered pain in the fellowship of the

local church. There are those who have chosen to bury their hurts. Others have resigned in frustration. Some mutter, 'What else could we expect?' This 'survivor's guide' doesn't offer easy answers, but asks a different set of questions. It thus makes a tremendously valuable contribution to church life.

In this sympathetic and sensitive book, James and Nina Rye carefully combine biblical teaching and practical experience. They bring into the open those questions which we all may prefer to ask in secret – yet reading their book is not a negative experience. They make an honest investigation of church life and how to survive it. They invite us to join in their exploration of what the church can and should become.

If we are to spend eternity together one day, then most of us need to get into practice here on earth. I trust that you will find reading these pages to be a real blessing – to you, your family and your church.

Clive Calver
General Director, Evangelical Alliance

PREFACE

This is a book about a sensitive subject. We have tried to bring a biblical perspective to bear on real problems. To enable us to discuss concrete church situations, we have chosen to construct characters and scenarios to illustrate points. Our creations are based on 'reality', but readers who try to identify churches or people from them are wasting time.

We are grateful to several friends who have read and commented on the typescript. We would like especially to acknowledge the help we have received from Jo Bramwell at IVP who has encouraged the book from its conception, and from a team of anonymous readers who have helped us walk through minefields. Where we have failed, the fault is ours.

Our aim has been to help, not cause offence. We have drawn from our own experience of the joys and pains of church life, and from our mistakes. We write as those who are still travelling, and not as those who have arrived.

King's Lynn   *James and Nina Rye*
January 1992

CHAPTER 1

THE GOOD
AND THE BAD

To live above with saints we love –
That really will be glory.
To live below with saints we know –
Well, that's another story!

Churches *can* be really helpful, can't they?

You may be able to think back to specific times when churches gave you the chance to think through doctrinal issues that you probably wouldn't have faced up to by yourself. Perhaps you can recall times of moving worship when you knew that God was present in an extraordinary way. There may have been many acts of sacrifice, compassion, and care, when people shared with you their cars, their money, their meals, their homes, their time, their prayers, and their tissues. Churches have probably given you some of the most rewarding and satisfying moments of your life so far. At its best, the body of Christ succeeds in bringing Jesus to its members, as well as to non-Christians.

But we also know that churches aren't always inspiring or helpful organizations. Even if the building is warm, we sometimes dread going to meetings because of the 'cold atmosphere', or because of the row that took place during the previous week.

Just like you

Joan was in her early fifties. She sat in our living room at 11 p.m., trying to come to terms with what had happened that evening at a church business meeting.

She had been with fellow Christians who were committed to building Christ's church. She had prayed about a particular matter for several days and had talked to wise counsellors. But she came to us bruised from running into 'a brick wall', feeling as if it had fallen on top of her. Her suggestions were met with opposition. Out of the blue, someone had said something which came across as an unjustified attack. Joan had lost her temper and things had been said which would take a long time to repair. The church rejected her proposals. She did not sleep that night. The ache lasted for months.

Wouldn't it be wonderful if everyone in your church was just like you? Think of the hours of 'full and frank' discussions that you could save. Just imagine it. Everybody would share your choice of skirt or shirt, jacket or jumper. Everyone would do exactly what you did with your hands during worship (straight up or straight down, pocketed or at half-mast). And everyone would share your considered and deeply held views on such topics as

- the extent of the body to be covered by water in baptism; and whether or not the recipient can be blessed, regardless of understanding;
- the importance, or otherwise, of candles, choirs, and clergy;

- the finer points of symbolism in the book of Revelation;
- the use of lawn-mowers on a Sunday;
- whether women should be allowed to wear dog collars;
- whether a 'simple gospel' service should be preached every week, or whether the 'gospel' should be regularly included as part of an on-going teaching ministry;
- the interpretation of Genesis 1–3 as a scientific, historical, or literary account of important events;
- whether confessing going to Spring Harvest is a sign of spiritual maturity, backsliding, or just plain insensitivity.

In our wiser moments it surely must come as a relief to realize that God doesn't want everybody in his church to be exactly like us. God has *far greater* ambitions for his people. He wants us to be like his Son. And even if we were all to become perfectly like Jesus before our death, churches would still be places where there would be considerable diversity.

There are some key issues over which Christians have genuinely disagreed for centuries. In some cases the differences are caused by our imperfect human nature. We just don't understand enough about what the Bible is teaching, or we aren't mature enough to be able to love people who don't agree with us. (Differences over baptism, for example, would fall into this category.) In other cases differences are actually part of God's positive plan for the church. He allows us variety in how we do his will. (For example, differences over the expression of worship would fall into this category.)

Rich diversity and sinful division

Some of us can remember what life was like before computers. When they first appeared in offices, great claims were made about what their arrival would mean for work practices. Much mistrust accompanied these inanimate electronic chips. And as millions of inexperienced people began to use

13

the new machines, many mistakes were inevitably made. It became fashionable to blame the computer. The phrase 'computer error' somehow seemed to absolve the operator from any fault.

Obviously, a few machines were poorly made and were capable of doing exasperating things, but in the vast majority of cases, the fault lay elsewhere. A new phrase began to gain some currency – 'garbage in: garbage out'. The computer experts were trying to get across to naïve users that a computer is simply a machine which follows instructions. Imperfect instructions led to imperfect results.

Without wishing to deny what God can do with people, there is a sense in which churches are as good or bad as the 'garbage' in them. We will never find perfect churches because churches are built with imperfect human beings. And even if we found a sinless church, we would corrupt it straight away with the sin that we would bring to it.

In some cases there is diversity because churches are greenhouses and not chapels of rest. Because God will spend our lives conforming us to his Son, churches are bound to be places where people are at different stages of holiness and understanding.

Often there is division because we fail to hold truth humbly. All of us used to live in a spiritual smog. We were unable to understand spiritual truth. And then God lifted that haze and we understood enough to come to faith in Christ. But unfortunately we still 'see but a poor reflection' (1 Corinthians 13:12). Although our understanding of God will grow through our study and experience of him, we are fallible human beings and will never know all that we want to know this side of heaven. Of course, there are crucial doctrines about which all Christians would agree. Sincere Christians will always differ, however, over how to interpret and apply the Bible. We should be wary of claiming inspiration for all of our particular viewpoints, especially over matters which have divided Christians throughout the centuries. Paul, the great apostle and theologian, said: 'I know in part ...' (1 Corinthians 13:12). There will always be diversity because of different levels of understanding.

Some differences within and between churches arise from our God-given differences as his creatures. We seem to forget that the whole of creation testifies to God's delight in variety. Our God created both the ant and the elephant, the lamb and the lion. Even within one species there can be particularly striking variation, and human beings are no exception. Apart from variety because of sex, size, colour, age, and physical and mental abilities, all of us have unique personalities with our own likes and dislikes, and our preferences for doing things in certain ways.

If the church down the road conducts services in a way which is different from the way your own does, it doesn't necessarily mean that it is any better or worse than yours. We have to learn to accept the fact that 'different' doesn't always have to be 'right' or 'wrong': it can just be 'different'. Some people find that silence aids their worship; others find constant loud clashes of tambourines helpful. You can't argue that, by itself, one aid to worship is more sinful than the other. But you can acknowledge that these two groups of people have a God-given diversity in their united desire to worship him.

We (James and Nina) have been part of living and growing churches where the patterns of worship have variously included

■ incense, vestments, a set liturgy;
■ a forty-five minute sermon, no open prayer, three very old hymns;
■ lots of modern songs and choruses, each sung at least four times with clapping and dancing;
■ long periods of silence, no set order of service;
... and so on!

But none of these, we would submit, were essential to

the life of the churches or to their growth. Unfortunately, such traditions can loom so large that they end up rather obscuring everything else.

Paul had to straighten out the Colossians on precisely this point (Colossians 2:6 – 3:4). Revered customs can look very fine, but we must get them into perspective. At worst, they are a valueless collection of teachings which have nothing to do with Christ at all; at best, they are still only a shadow of the reality found in Christ. You may find some church traditions extremely difficult to cope with, but it is as well to remember that, while you worship, God looks on the heart.

From the beginning

We shouldn't look back to the New Testament church and think that if only we were alive then, our relationships would be perfect and our understanding would be complete. In some ways, the reality of the New Testament church is similar to our own. Paul had to plead with Euodia and Syntyche to agree (Philippians 4:2). He told the Ephesians: 'Get rid of all bitterness, rage and anger, brawling and slander, along with every form of malice' (Ephesians 4:31). He has to remind the Corinthians that love 'is not easily angered' and that 'it keeps no record of wrongs' (1 Corinthians 13:5). And Luke is honest enough to tell us that even Barnabas and Paul, who had known God's blessing on their joint ministry, 'had such a sharp disagreement that they parted company' (Acts 15:39). In the New Testament church, as now, there was sinful division.

In the New Testament we also find evidence of Christians growing in their understanding and of making mistakes. The differences between Jewish and Gentile Christians are a major concern of church life in the years immediately following the coming of the Holy Spirit. Christians from entirely different cultural backgrounds were being thrown together and a hot theological issue of the day was the extent to which Gentile converts should be expected to conform to aspects of the Jewish law.

Peter undergoes a major theological change after God sends him a vision in Joppa before he goes to visit Cornelius (Acts 10:9–20). He learns that he can eat with Gentiles and is reminded that God wants Gentiles to come into his kingdom without having to follow ceremonial aspects of Jewish law. Perhaps because of a combination of sinful thinking and sociological pressure, however, he later changes his views about what is required of Gentile converts. Paul has to rebuke him sharply (Galatians 2:11–13).

There is also evidence in the New Testament of Christians changing their practices. For example, the ruling of the Jerusalem Council that Gentile believers should refrain from eating food sacrificed to idols, blood, and the meat of strangled animals (Acts 15:29) is not universally accepted by the church today. When writing to the Corinthians at a later date, Paul had to give the church advice on such issues (1 Corinthians 8), and it is not known at what point Gentile Christians knowingly decided that this ruling no longer applied, and started to eat blood.

Another example is the practice that many believers had in the early days of keeping all things in common (Acts 2:44). This became less common as time went on, however, probably after the persecution of the church in Jerusalem.

Some New Testament Christians clearly had different religious practices from others. It is highly improbable that churches containing mainly Jewish Christians had worship identical to that of congregations of mainly Gentile believers. And Paul tells the Colossians that no-one is to judge them by what they 'eat or drink, or with regard to a religious festival, a New Moon celebration or a Sabbath day' (Colossians 2:16).

In church we experience both the sin of people and the

17

grace of God. The spiritual failure that we sometimes see appears all the more awful because it happens amongst people who ought to know better. And at times we want to give up and leave it, to lick our wounds in a quiet corner. We want to argue that God will understand and will not expect us to put up with it any more.

One of the key messages of this book is that God does expect us to put up with it. In fact, he expects more of us than that. He wants us to contribute positively to it. And the other important message is that there is hope for the church – yes, even your church – because the grace of God is greater than the sin of people, and his foolishness is wiser than our wisdom. Despite all the imperfections of the church, God, in his 'foolishness', has chosen it to be one of his most important means of caring for his people, and of extending his kingdom.

If we are to cope with church life, we need to remind ourselves of what the church is. That's the topic of the next two chapters.

CHAPTER 2

WHAT'S THE CHURCH ABOUT?

The church on the spot

The word 'church' today conjures up all sorts of images and ideas, from stained glass windows to huddles of people with black Bibles. The Greek word the New Testament writers used was *ekklēsia*. This had the meaning of 'assembly' or 'meeting together', rather as 'congregation' has in English.[1] Our Bible versions translate it as 'church'.

After the Day of Pentecost, the followers of Jesus in Jerusalem began meeting together. They became known later as 'the church in Jerusalem'. Other groups of Christians in other areas met together too, as the gospel spread. Each group became known as a 'church'.

Many of Paul's 'letter openers' illustrate what he meant by a 'church'. Here are a few of them:

'To all in Rome who are loved by God and called to be saints' (Romans 1:7).

'To the church of God in Corinth, to those sanctified in Christ Jesus and called to be holy, together with all those everywhere who call on the name of our Lord Jesus Christ – their Lord and ours' (1 Corinthians 1:2).

'To all the saints in Christ Jesus at Philippi, together with the overseers and deacons' (Philippians 1:1). (But We're sure the overseers and deacons were saints too!)

'To the holy and faithful brothers in Christ at Colosse' (Colossians 1:2).

Even from these 'one-liners', we get the picture of a church as a family which was so intimately related to God that it was 'in him', and also like him ('holy' and 'faithful'). Paul's words, written in the first century, remind us, in the late twentieth, that a local church is not a building, the clergy or a pastoral team; nor is it elders, deacons, PCC or administrative group. It is not even an inner circle of signed-on-the-sacred-dotted-line members. It is, quite simply and inclusively, all the believers who meet together in that congregation.

Picture a church

If you were to stand at the front of an average Sunday morning congregation, what would you see? How would you describe it? Might you do as Jesus did, when he talked about his people?[2] He used a wide range of word pictures, including seeds and soils, crops and weeds, a vine, treasure, yeast, fish and flocks of sheep. Clearly he foresaw that his people would be weedy, sheepish and a very mixed catch! Equally, he knew they would have tremendous potential for growth, glorifying God and turning the world upside-down.

He also regarded his people, more intimately, as his family: 'Whoever does God's will is my brother and my sister and my mother' (Mark 3:35). After his resurrection, Jesus spoke of 'my Father and your Father' (John 20:17). Jesus taught that his followers are, in him, a family together. People who become Christians are joined, not only to Christ, but also to all his other relatives. They are adopted into his family.

The same picture is taken up in the New Testament letters. Christians are 'the family of believers' (Galatians 6:10) and 'adopted as [God the Father's] sons' (Ephesians 1:5). Paul begins his prayer for the Ephesians with these words: 'For this reason I kneel before the Father, from whom his whole family in heaven and on earth derives its name.' (Ephesians 3:14–15). So yes, those Christians at church are your relations in Christ!

Both children and adults need families. Individuals cannot be families. The moment people are forgiven by Jesus Christ and start to follow him as Lord they begin a unique relationship with him. They also join the family of God. Each child of God needs other Christians, not just in a loose or general sense, but in a setting that provides family togetherness. This, we believe, is what a local church is meant to provide.

Peter and Paul also used other word pictures to describe the young churches, including

■ the body of Christ (*e.g.* 1 Corinthians 12:27);
■ a building, and also a temple for the Holy Spirit (*e.g.* 1 Peter 2:4–5; Ephesians 2:21–22);
■ an army (*e.g.* Ephesians 6:12);
■ an olive tree with both wild and cultivated branches (Romans 11:17–24). (This might describe a church you know!)

A church is obviously a complex thing, to lend itself to such varying metaphors. Note, however, the implication common to each one: that Christians need to work together and fit together. The individual Christian is meant to be part of something bigger to fulfil and to experience all that God has in store. That 'something bigger' is a local church.

What does a church do?

The old joke has it that churches are for 'hatches, matches and despatches'. But strangely, Luke wrote about none of these in his descriptions of early church life. In Acts 2:41–47, we find the first account of the young church in Jerusalem. Luke tells us that God's family met together, shared a special meal together, prayed and sang together, learned from God together and shared their homes and possessions. Unsurprisingly, verse 44 sums it up in the words, 'All the believers were together.'

This passage actually contains nineteen facts about the church at that time. Five of these are still considered to be essential for a Christian church today. They are

- baptism (verse 41),
- teaching (verse 42),
- the special breaking of bread meal (verses 42 and 46),
- prayer (verses 42 and 47),
- fellowship (verses 42, 44–46).

We leave you to pick out the other fourteen facts and decide which of them happen in your church today. Aren't some of them just as essential as the 'big five'?

The big five

1. Baptism

Jesus himself commanded believers to be baptized. 'Therefore go and make disciples of all nations, baptising them in the name of the Father and of the Son and of the Holy Spirit, and teaching them to obey everything I have commanded you' (Matthew 28:19–20). From the Day of Pentecost onwards, Christians have been baptized, to signify publicly their commitment to the Lord Jesus Christ.

Just as a wedding ring is a symbol of the promises to be faithful and committed in the marriage partnership, so baptism is a symbol too. There are different traditions in the churches regarding baptism now, but we can say that it is a symbol of the grace of God which looks forwards or backwards to a spiritual birth and cleansing from sin. (See chapter 5 for a fuller discussion of baptism.)

Part of the symbolic significance is also that it shows that a person *belongs* in God's family. Both baptism and the Lord's supper are about belonging. Both have been practised from earliest times and are recognized in some form in virtually every branch of Christianity today.

2. The Lord's supper (also called holy communion, the breaking of bread, the eucharist)

This special meal, where Christians share bread and wine together, was established by Jesus the night before he died. The broken bread symbolizes Christ's broken body; the wine symbolizes his poured-out blood (Matthew 26:26–29; Mark 14:22–25; Luke 22:19–20). The Lord's supper commemorates the fact that Jesus was punished so that we can be forgiven; it also looks forward to his return (1 Corinthians 11:23–26). As we eat and drink together it is another reminder that we are part of one whole. Jesus does not want us to forget how we belong to him *and* to each other. The two things go together.

3. Teaching

The first Christians 'devoted themselves to the apostles' teaching' (Acts 2:42), which is preserved for us in the New

Testament. Their teaching came from three inter-related sources:

- the apostles' own experience of Christ's life, work and teaching;
- the Old Testament, which Jesus Christ regarded as authoritative;

and, breathing through both of these,

- the Holy Spirit himself, as Jesus had promised them: 'The Counsellor, the Holy Spirit, whom the Father will send in my name, will teach you all things and will remind you of everything I have said to you' (John 14:26).[3]

The apostle Paul tells us: 'All Scripture is God-breathed and is useful for teaching, rebuking, correcting and training in righteousness' (2 Timothy 3:16), so the Bible must be *the* source book for all teaching in churches.

Even at the beginning there was a danger that doctrinal error would creep into congregations. Many of the New Testament letters were written to combat this danger. A church clearly has a responsibility to obey Paul's instructions to Timothy: 'Preach the Word; be prepared in season and out of season; correct, rebuke and encourage – with great patience and careful instruction' (2 Timothy 4:2). Churches have to both guard and proclaim biblical truth.

Clearly, you don't have to go to church to receive teaching. The Holy Spirit can help your understanding as you read the Bible by yourself. He can even use Christian books! However, the local church should provide a more complete programme of teaching than you might choose for yourself – thorny issues as well as safe topics. This need not be all by sermons either: congregations include people who, given the opportunity, can help you informally, by sharing their own problems, insights, and successes.

4. Prayer

No-one would dispute that prayer should be an important part of every Christian's life. Jesus himself spent much time in prayer;[4] he taught his disciples how to pray too.[5] But do Christians really need to pray *together*, as well as privately?

There are over twenty references in Acts to prayer and praying. Almost all speak of believers praying together, as a church. There is a strong case for saying that many of the events of the book of Acts are answers to the prayers made at a church prayer meeting in Acts 4. The believers joined together and, after reminding themselves of God's greatness, prayed: 'Enable your servants to speak your words with great boldness. Stretch out your hand to heal and perform miraculous signs and wonders through the name of your holy servant Jesus' (Acts 4:29–30). And that's just what happened.

Prayer can take many forms: worship and praise (sung and spoken), asking, listening, pleading and interceding, confession and also simply telling God about something. Prayer is one of the church's greatest privileges and also part of its work of building God's kingdom.

5. Fellowship

If all churches got this one right, there would probably be no need for this book!

We all know that fellowship is something to do with sharing, but the idea has become rather debased among many Christians today. It is too often watered down to mean simply 'talking together'. Important as this is (!), originally it also meant something more solid. Fellowship in New Testament churches involved people sharing in three ways.[6]

a. Sharing in spiritual realities
People who have fellowship all share in the reality of Christ. They all participate in the same Lord and enjoy being joined

to Jesus.[7] This is most tangibly evident at a communion service: 'Is not the cup of thanksgiving for which we give thanks a participation in the blood of Christ? And is not the bread that we break a participation in the body of Christ?' (1 Corinthians 10:16). This fellowship brings an awareness of 'togetherness'.

b. Sharing in an experience (such as suffering)

In the first century, the fellowship of shared experiences was often during times of suffering and persecution, as Paul wrote: 'Our hope for you is firm, because we know that just as you share in our sufferings, so also you share in our comfort' (2 Corinthians 1:7). But other shared experiences can also lead to this kind of fellowship. For instance, people who work together at something for the Lord share the joys, frustrations, agonies and triumphs in a direct way. As you have probably realized, there is all the difference in the world between organizing and participating in a youth camp and just hearing about it afterwards!

Shared experiences forge bonds and encourage deeper friendships. Involvement in a local church ought to give plenty of opportunity for this kind of fellowship.

c. Sharing material possessions

Luke writes about a very practical form of fellowship: 'No-one claimed that any of his possessions was his own, but they shared everything they had' (Acts 4:32). Somehow it sounds too good to be true! Yet we (James and Nina) have seen many examples of just this kind of loving attitude among Christians we know: garden tools lent out, cars exchanged for family holidays, large sums of money given freely, ovens and toasters mended ... the list could go on and on. Paul writes fully on the privilege of giving willingly to help other Christians (2 Corinthians 8:1–9:15), and it *is* a privilege to give or to receive this kind of fellowship.

26

At this point you may be wondering why we have given so much attention to the one subject, fellowship, in comparison with the other four in this section. We want to underscore the fact that true Christian fellowship is something more than a cup of tea and a biscuit at the end of a service or meeting! It is also more than 'fellowship', a warm feeling. Fellowship is rooted in spiritual reality, yet it is intensely practical; it should not be cut and dried, or restricted to certain settings or occasions, but should arise out of shared activities and experiences.

The experience of fellowship among Christians is certainly not confined to 'church occasions', but it would be worrying if it were never encountered there! Christians who are fully part of their local church can participate in fellowship in many ways, as God intends they should.

In our worse moments, we may be tempted to think that God is a miserable person in the sky who plans how to make life inconvenient for Christians. ('Fancy wanting *me* to go to *that* church!') Of course, such a view of God's motives is a travesty of the truth. God cares so much about us that he sent Jesus to save us. And having given us his Son, he is not about to work against us once we have become Christians. Despite what we may be tempted to think on occasions, God called the church into being in order to *help* Christians. He created churches as a means of strengthening us in our faith and as a means of helping us to serve him.

Each one of the 'big five' things we have considered in this chapter is part of God's love gift to his children. But God is so compassionate that even these five things cannot adequately describe what he intended us to experience in the local church. We continue to explore the New Testament picture of the church in the next chapter.

CHAPTER 3

YET MORE!

There are other important elements in church life that we have not yet dealt with. We hope you won't be too disappointed that the PCC, trust deeds and cleaning rotas are not mentioned (necessary though these are)! The five issues we think we should explore (if only briefly) are

- correction and discipline;
- comfort and encouragement;
- evangelism;
- love;
- meeting for worship.

Correction and discipline

'We all stumble in many ways. If anyone is never at fault in what he says, he is a perfect man, able to keep his whole body in check' (James 3:2). But wouldn't it be tragic if no-one ever helped us up from our stumbles? Of if we were allowed to go on in our faults unchecked, with no-one prepared to help us find a better way?

No-one enjoys being pulled up and corrected, but we all need it from time to time. It is best and most often done privately and informally. A close friend may help you to see what you are doing and encourage you to change your wrong attitudes or actions; someone may preach a sermon or share an insight which brings God's word right to your doorstep, and you receive it as correction from the Lord; or perhaps someone writes to you or lends you a book, with the same result. Formal church discipline is necessary only when you persist, unrepentant, in some specific way that is clearly contrary to biblical teaching (Matthew 18:15–20).

Although some churches misuse discipline to punish a repentant sinner, the biblical emphasis is on restoration. A key passage is Galatians 6:1–10, in which Paul writes, sensitively yet firmly, to advise both would-be correctors and those in need of correction: pride and assumed righteousness must have no place; the motives must be to do good and to please the Holy Spirit; the attitudes on both sides should be loving, caring and humble. Strange as it may seem, one of the best things about belonging to a church is that you can be lovingly corrected, should you need it.

Comfort and encouragement

We all need people to encourage us to go on loving and following Jesus, both directly in words, and by example. When Christianity is real and not just pious pretence, churches are places where believers give comfort and encouragement to each other. As with correction and discipline, the motives should spring from love and humility, not a secret desire to 'crow' or boast.

But have you noticed the law of 'reverse encouragement'? It states two things. First, if you try to encourage by saying how marvellous everything is for you and ignore the reality of others' lives, it can be discouraging for your hearers. Secondly, sharing your own difficulties can sometimes be a help to others.

Tom: I had *such* a wonderful 'quiet time' this morning. I was in prayer for well over an hour, and in my Bible reading the Lord gave me a real word from himself. Isn't God gracious?

Jim (thinks to himself): Of course he is. But I feel so guilty and inferior, comparing myself to this super-Christian. Perhaps every other Christian is like him and I am the odd one out. I don't feel encouraged at all. I even fail to be wholeheartedly glad for my friend, which makes me worse still!

Sally: Isn't it devastating when you realize how difficult it is to forgive your parents for the way they brought you up? I thought it would be easier for a Christian, but just now I'm finding the exact opposite.

Carol (thinks to herself): What a relief. Here is someone like me, someone who has problems. It's so encouraging to find a person who is willing to be honest. I might be able to talk about things that matter with this person.

Many Christian people desperately need encouragement and comfort. A caring church fellowship is the best place to receive the genuine article.[1]

Evangelism

Jesus' commission to 'go and make disciples of all nations' (Matthew 28:19–20) leaves us in no doubt that he means us so to live, work and bear witness that people will turn to him and follow him. But there is no blueprint given as to how evangelism must be done.

Reading the New Testament, we discover that people became followers of Jesus in a variety of circumstances:

- in response to 'life-style evangelism'
  (*e.g.* Acts 2:47, soon after the Day of Pentecost);
- by attending 'house meetings'
  (*e.g.* Acts 10:24–48, Cornelius with his relatives and close friends);
- by attending 'open airs'
  (*e.g.* Acts 16:13–14, Lydia by the river);
- by attending religious services and hearing about Jesus
  (*e.g.* Acts 14:1, in the synagogue);
- by finding themselves, although unaware of it at the time, in the right place at God's time
  (*e.g.* Acts 16:29–34, the Philippian jailor and his family).

Evangelism could be formal or informal, planned or opportunistic, because Christians were ready to speak and to act, and to give the Holy Spirit freedom to work. Bringing people to Jesus was not something added on to the life of the church, it was integral to it. The life of the Spirit showed itself in the church as the people shared the heart of God. Because Jesus came to seek and to save the lost, evangelism has to be one of the central tasks of the churches.

Of course, you do not have to be part of a church to engage in evangelism in its full sense. But in practice it is often the local church that provides the training and impetus that encourage you to go ahead and do it. Also, the churches we read about in the New Testament did not aim simply to get people to 'make decisions', as we so often do today. Converts were instructed to repent and be baptized. Paul laboured to see everyone 'perfect in Christ' (Colossians 1:28, 29). New believers need the context of the local church, with all that it has to offer, in order to grow in Christ.

Love

Churches should be loving communities. It is tragic that prominent elements in the lives of a few churches include back-biting, envy, snobbery, gossip and other forms of 'hate thy neighbour'. Jesus gave his disciples a new command: 'Love one another. As I have loved you, so you must love one another. By this all men will know that you are my disciples, if you love one another' (John 13:34–35). To love each other as God loves us, that is a high standard. But when we do, people notice.

First-century believers did not live under a magic cloud of *agapē* that protected them from all those nasty impulses the rest of us have. On the contrary, they struggled just as much, as the letters to the churches show. John's first letter keeps on coming back to the central message, 'We should love one another' (1 John 3:11). He and the other apostles gave specific teaching about unconditional love for brothers and sisters in Christ. They did not hesitate to use the real names for the opposite; for example, favouritism (James 2:1–13), covetousness (James 4:2), malice (1 Peter 2:1), bitterness (Ephesians 4:31), murder (1 John 3:12).

It can be very hard for people in a church to love each other. After all, some people there would not choose each other as friends in a million years. But they *will* be spending eternity together! Unless they take seriously this command to love each other, it is questionable whether their church has a future (see Revelation 2:1–5). Peter sums it up like this: 'Above all, love each other deeply, because love covers over a multitude of sins' (1 Peter 4:8).

Sometimes, we are tempted to push aside the centrality of love, focusing instead on what we *do*. But this is to ignore what is important to God.

> I may go to a lively church where the gifts of the Spirit are splendidly evident in us all.

32

I may go to a very sound church where the doctrines of grace are preached and revered.
I may go to a church that sacrificially gives away 20% of its income to Tear Fund and missionary support.
I may go to a church that is deeply involved in local community aid projects.
I may go to a church that observes reverently all the ceremonies, the special days and the right way of doing things.
I may give every spare waking moment to working for the church I attend.
But

> if I lose my love-relationship with God,
> if I do not love the people in my church,

what do I have?

(Compare 1 Corinthians 13)

In our search for a biblical answer to the question 'What's the church about?' we have looked at 'the essentials', but unconditional love, like that which the Lord has for us, must permeate everything.

Meeting for worship

A very wise and godly Christian wrote to a church once: 'Let us not give up meeting together, as some are in the habit of doing, but let us encourage one another – and all the more as you see the Day approaching' (Hebrews 10:25).

It seems that, even in New Testament times, some followers of Jesus Christ wanted to opt out of church life. The counsel they received – 'Don't give up' – is still good today.

The passage in Hebrews containing the advice is all about communal worship. It is exciting and challenging to discover what *should* characterize our meeting together.

Confidence (10:19–20, 22)

Together we can come very close to God through and in Jesus Christ. We don't have to question our worthiness to be there, or God's desire to have us. We can approach with boldness. God wants us to draw close to him as a congregation.

Sincerity (10:21–22)

We don't have to play-act or try to hide guilty secrets. We can be honest and open. We know that God knows what we are really like. Because of our faith in Jesus' death and resurrection we have assurance of forgiveness.

A hold on the biblical doctrine that underpins faith (10:23)

We need not give up when our emotions pull us down, nor swerve to avoid the obstacles to faith that arise, such as illness, depression, bereavement, natural and unnatural disasters. Meeting together should help us to become strong in our understanding of God's character.

Practical and visible demonstration of love (10:24)

When it is hard to love the unlovely, meeting together will provide frequent opportunities for being a servant. Also, as we see others living like Jesus, they will be an encouragement to us, helping us as we try to show love that is real.

Giving and receiving encouragement and support (10:25)

As the day of judgment gets closer, we should be increasingly concerned to be ready for it. Far from being an outmoded form of Christian commitment, meeting together for worship is more and more necessary. When we worship together, we can support and encourage each other.

Isn't communal worship like this worth having, worth praying for and worth working towards? By opting out we would be missing out on all these benefits, encouragements and opportunities to make God's own heart glad. So let's not opt out of church, when God so clearly wants us to opt in.

So far we've tried to take a look at what the church is. In the rest of the book we want to continue to argue that Christians should be committed to church involvement (despite real difficulties), and we want to give positive, practical advice for dealing with problems that can arise.

CHAPTER 4

DIFFERENCES OVER THE FAMILY RULE BOOK

As we are often painfully aware, not everyone in the church will always agree with us. Some differences that exist between members of the Christian family are obvious. Visiting the nearest church on holiday can lead to 'culture shock', especially for the children. 'Dad, why did they ...? And why did they ...? *We* don't do that! Dad, why don't we?'

But other differences are much more subtle. For example, most Christians would claim to 'believe' in the Bible. It is appealed to, with varying degrees of conviction, as an authoritative source for teaching on doctrine and practice. Christians interpret it, however, in widely differing ways.

Not all Christians would totally agree with our own view that the Bible is God's unique revealed truth. We don't believe in the infallibility of any particular translation. We are acutely aware that we don't always fully understand the text (have you ever tried to preach on Zechariah 12?), and that we differ between ourselves as to which parts of the Bible God wants us to take as history, and which parts as literature. But we are committed to an evangelical view of the Bible. We believe that the original words of both the Old and New Testaments were inspired by God, and that the Bible is wholly reliable in both fact and doctrine. What the Bible says, God says.

In this chapter we consider some of the different stances that Christians have taken about believing and obeying the Bible. Please don't make the mistake of thinking that because we describe the views that some have taken, we are necessarily endorsing them ourselves. We are simply trying to promote a critical awareness of the variety of opinion that exists within the church.

I believe in the Bible

Some Christians claim to believe that every word in the Bible is to be taken literally. For example, they understand the opening chapters of Genesis as a record of scientific fact; they don't doubt that Job was an historical figure; they argue that women should have their heads covered in public worship because of Paul's commands to the Corinthian church. They also argue that, as the Word of God, the Bible (or their interpretation of it), takes precedence over human reason and the church's traditions in questions of doctrine and behaviour. A common label for such a position is 'fundamentalism'.

Others argue that the Bible *contains* the word of God, but that as it stands, it also contains error of fact. They argue that parts of it (such as the Levitical laws) are clearly not at all relevant today. Although it may contain interesting ideas about God, and the way people thought about God, it cannot be regarded as completely authoritative revelation. People should accept those parts which they find helpful. Much of the historical information is rejected or understood as fable; the miraculous is regarded as impossible. On these premises, it would clearly be folly to regard Scripture as the Christian's supreme authority in matters of belief and behaviour. Rather, Scripture must be 'sifted' by reason. Common labels for such a position are 'liberalism' or 'modernism'.

Between those two extremes (which to some extent are caricatures) there is a wide range of opinion. We suspect that most readers of this book would fall a lot closer to fundamentalism than to liberalism. If you imagine a continuum from A to Z, with the extreme fundamentalist being A, and the extreme liberal being Z, most evangelical Christians would fall somewhere between A and about J.

Two overlapping factors have contributed to these different views of the Bible.

First, we now have a greater knowledge about the world (through science and history) than was available to writers of the Bible and to readers in previous generations. This has led people to question certain aspects of the Bible, and this, in turn, has led to differences among Christians. In previous centuries, for instance, Christians argued that the Bible taught that the sun moved round the earth. Since the views of Copernicus (that the earth travels round the sun) were demonstrated to be true, however, we have been forced to re-evaluate the biblical passages our Christian predecessors felt so certain about.

Secondly, the use of human reason as the judge of revelation has also led to differences between Christians. There have always been those who would have doubted the truth of the Bible. But the Enlightenment, with the *belief* that human reason is the measure of all truth, made such doubts more acceptable for many.

Take the question of biblical miracles as an example. Scientists have spent many years trying to discover laws which govern the universe. They conduct experiments, observe and analyse data, and then formulate hypotheses which can, in turn, be tested empirically. It is argued that because the miracles would have contradicted scientific knowledge of how the universe runs, they could not have happened. They are explained as inventions of over-zealous writers, parables to teach important truth, or naïve accounts of events which have a perfectly rational explanation.

Strengths and weaknesses

There are clearly strengths and weaknesses in both liberalism and fundamentalism.

Liberals have been helpful in pointing out awkward issues in the biblical text that most fundamentalists in the pews have been unaware of, or unwilling to face. For example, liberals have drawn attention to the fact that the Bible *appears* to contradict itself on occasions. In Matthew 23:35, whose son is Zechariah? There appears to be confusion between the murdered son of Jehoiada (2 Chronicles 24:20–22) and the earlier Zechariah whose father was, indeed, Berakiah. And does Mark give the wrong reference to 'the days of Abiathar the high priest' (Mark 2:26)? It certainly *looks* initially as if the correct name should have been Ahimelech, as described in 1 Samuel 21:1–6.

Liberals are also quick to point out that the biblical writers often wrote their accounts according to standards of ancient rather than modern history. The gospel writers frequently quote prophets, but sometimes their identification initially *appears* inaccurate. For example, Mark quotes Malachi and Isaiah (Mark 1:2–3), but attributes both quotations to Isaiah.

Perhaps the greatest weakness of liberalism is its presuppositions. Liberals approach the Bible presuming that they have the authority to judge it. They are committed to the Bible only in so far as they agree with it or judge it to be reasonable. Many liberals approach the Bible in the same way that some people share meals, with one person bringing the main course, and somebody else bringing the second course – the author brings the words and the reader the meaning. To approach the Bible with the assumption that miracles or predictive prophecy couldn't happen suggests that God cannot intervene in history and it denies much of the intended meaning. Liberals want to submit to God by submitting to what they find acceptable in his revelation. Many would argue that such thinking is humanistic rather than Christian.

The main strength of fundamentalism is its commitment to the authority of the Bible. Fundamentalists accept that revelation sometimes confounds and judges reason, and that the foolishness of God is greater than the wisdom of people. They believe what the Bible says about itself, that people 'spoke from God' (Hebrews 1:1; 2 Peter 1:21). This is confirmed by Christ's use of the Old Testament as God speaking, and by the early church's acceptance of the New Testament writings. Fundamentalists want to submit to God by submitting to the Bible.

Fundamentalism lays itself open to two main criticisms. The first is that in stressing the 'divine nature' of the Bible, it can fail to take adequate account of its 'human nature' – the influence of the personalities and times of the writers on what was written. Fundamentalists sometimes give the impression that they think 'inspiration' means that God dictated the Scriptures and that the human writers merely acted as perfect mechanical typewriters, without influencing their content. But God didn't do this. He chose to speak through people who had personalities of their own, and who were living in a particular epoch. Paul's letters, for example, were written with specific situations in mind. The letter to the Philippians is different in tone and content from the first letter to the Corinthians because the churches are different. The Holy Spirit inspired and used Paul's knowledge of these churches. And Paul's personality and background show themselves in the letters in a variety of ways; including his outbursts of praise (Ephesians 3:20–21), anger (Philippians 3:2), and his use of a rabbinic method of argument (Galatians 3:15–25).

This doesn't mean the Bible is therefore fallible. But it does mean that we need to understand what the words meant to the people at the time before we can apply them to ourselves. And if the cultural circumstances have changed, it may not be possible to follow the words literally today. The book of Leviticus is an important part of the Bible, but its application to us today cannot be the same as it was for the original readers.

If we take the line that every word in the Bible should be taken as literally true, we end up with tremendous problems. If we ignore the fact that different types of writing have different conventions, poetry will be seen as history and we will think that robes washed in blood should come out white (Revelation 7:14). We would even gouge out people's eyes or cut off their hands if we failed to appreciate that, in the literary culture of the time, it was perfectly normal to exaggerate to achieve an effect (Matthew 5:29–30). If we felt compelled to take every statement as scientifically or historically true (even if there is really good evidence to the contrary), we would fail to appreciate the communication skill of the supreme botanist. When Jesus said that the mustard seed was the smallest seed (Matthew 13:32) he was not making a 'scientifically true' statement, but was adapting his message to the known world of the time.

The second criticism of fundamentalism is the inconsistency of its followers. Many fundamentalists, who profess to follow the Bible without cultural interpretation, are still selective about which parts they obey literally and which others they reinterpret. One can understand why they worship on a Sunday rather than the Sabbath, and can appreciate why they baptize rather than circumcise. According to their premises, however, it is difficult to understand fundamentalists who don't stone those caught in adultery, greet one another with a kiss, raise their hands in worship, or regularly wash one another's feet.

The balloon, the parrot, and the kite

John Stott's parable is useful here. He describes[1] the liberal as a gas-filled balloon and the fundamentalist as a caged bird. The liberal mind is accountable only to itself in its thinking and application of the Bible and is therefore blown about without any anchorage. The fundamentalist mind has the God-given capacity to think and apply the Bible, but it is bound by unhelpful traditions and conventions.

The kite, by contrast, is free to fly high, but it is also anchored very firmly to the ground. Its freedom to fly has well-defined limitations. Evangelicals are not simply midway between fundamentalists and liberals. They share the fundamentalist's strong concern to submit to the Bible as God's inerrant revelation. They are firmly tied to the ground of biblical inspiration and authority.

In order to submit to the authority of God's revelation more fully, however, evangelicals wish to use their God-given minds to understand and interpret it appropriately. Although they may differ over the precise details of interpretation of particular passages, they are in broad agreement that the Bible contains no inconsistencies, that any apparent contradictions can be resolved, or will be resolved as our knowledge of ancient languages and cultures increases, and that the Bible is clear in the message it gives us about God.

Despite being written by many authors over a large time-scale, all the books of the Bible are consistent in the view they present of God as a Creator, loving Saviour, and Judge, who works to save fallen human beings.

The dangers of ballooning

In an age when many people have grown up in a culture which promotes lies about the Bible (for instance, that it is full of errors), not everybody who comes to faith in Christ is able to adopt an evangelical position on the Bible immediately. They will need time to get to know it for themselves and may need to study the doctrine of inspiration more closely. Other Christians perhaps came to faith with a fundamentalist view of the Bible but now feel they have escaped from their cage. Those who fail (for whatever reason) to see the Bible as God's authoritative and infallible revelation to the human race face several problems. There isn't space here to discuss these at length. But one major intellectual problem and one major spiritual difficulty must be mentioned.

Those Christians who reject the inspiration and authority of the Bible are clearly being inconsistent. They want to believe in God, but dismiss parts of the documents which report his intervention in history and reveal his character. Their faith clearly has little foundation outside of themselves. And if they claim that they believe in Jesus, they will find it difficult to answer the critic who says: 'But *why* do you? He is revealed in a book which you claim is unreliable in parts. Why are the parts you believe in more reliable than the parts you reject? What you regard as reliable one day might become unreliable on the next day according to your whim. And how can you say you believe in Jesus when you clearly disbelieve something that he taught – namely the inspiration of the Old Testament?'

A major spiritual difficulty faced by these people is

that of pride. Spiritual growth is often characterized by a willingness to accept that we are wrong, and by a turning to accept God's judgment about a situation and a desire to follow his will. Those who reject the authority and inspiration of the Bible have become their own gods, determining which parts of revelation are true or false. If we reject those messages which do not fit our view of what God is like, we will never grow in our understanding of him, and that will affect our spirituality.

Living with differences about the Bible

Here are three tips for handling differences about the Bible with other Christians.

Accept your brothers and sisters

In the New Testament church there were those who said that in order to be a Christian you needed to put your faith in Christ *and* keep all the Jewish law. Paul wrote the letter to the Galatians to argue against such a heresy. Don't make the arrogant mistake of insisting that somebody has to share your particular view of every Bible passage, on top of having faith in Christ, in order to be part of God's family. You may even find yourself sitting next to them in a hundred years' time in the Heavenly Theological College. The family bond should be more important than the weakness of understanding on both sides.

Don't be simplistic or lazy

The Bible isn't a systematic theology, and at times can be extremely difficult to interpret. Respect the difficulties that those who differ from you may be having and avoid making gross generalizations about their faith on the basis of a few statements. (We know of one preacher who was severely taken to task at the end of a service because he dared to use his knowledge of Hebrew to question the translation of a word in the Authorized Version!) Recognize that the arguments involved may be complex, and that people may change their positions and appear inconsistent as they wrestle with issues. If we are to grow in knowledge, we may have to change our minds on occasions.

Don't be defeated into thinking that the problems in understanding the Bible are unanswerable. But don't expect the answers to come in visions. You'll almost certainly have to consult evangelical commentaries.

See elephants as elephants and nits as nits

The fact that someone doesn't share your views on Adam and Eve, or your interpretation of verses in 1 Timothy 2, may make you shake with rage, or almost burst with a sense of spiritual superiority. But such differences are not necessarily the most important ones.

You can differ with people over these issues and still share a common respect for the Bible and a desire to submit to it. The major difference is with those who do not accept the authority of the Bible, who feel free to cut out difficult parts of it, and who do not accept the Bible's teaching about its own inspiration (not least, the teaching of Christ himself).

You should find it possible to remain part of a church which clearly respects the Bible and teaches it systematically, even if you disagree with particular interpretations on secondary issues. We see little point, however, in remaining in a church that does not really accept the authority of the Bible and only pays lip-service to serious biblical exposition. You should feel no compunction about leaving a church where central Christian truths (such as the deity of Christ, the physical resurrection of Christ, and justification by faith) are denied. If you are to devote yourself to the apostles' teaching, you need to be in a church where there is a reasonable chance that it will be recognized and faithfully taught.

The Bible is a mixture of a letter from a father and a Highway Code. Don't become so embroiled in using it as a game for scoring points against your opponents that you fail to be thrilled by its message of love and ignore its commandments for life. Let's devote our energy to putting into practice what we clearly know to be true, instead of being guilty of spending too much time worrying about how others don't agree with us.

Problems in the park

Imagine the scene. It's a glorious autumn day, with enough wind to fly kites. Four children from the same family are in the park together, each with their own wind-loving possession. After half-an-hour what are they doing? You've guessed it. Fighting! Fighting about the right way to fly wood and plastic, and about which one mum and dad like best!

We continue our discussion about differences between Christians in the next chapter.

CHAPTER 5

CROSSING SOME BARRICADES

Murder in the family?

In the early part of the sixteenth century a man called Felix Manz was executed in Switzerland. He wasn't a thief or a murderer. He just happened to hold different views about baptism from those of the ruling religious authorities.[1] Tragically, many others shared a similar fate. You may be able to guess what views Manz held from the fact that drowning was chosen as the method of execution.

Although we may no longer execute, with public approval, Christians who have practices different from our own, we may have held other Christians in contempt because of these differences. In extreme cases, we may have been guilty of murder (Matthew 5:21–26).

In this chapter we want to look at a few of the obvious issues that divide some Christians. Whatever our personal views on the topics covered, we need to try to understand why those across the divide practise what they do. We need to listen to our sisters and brothers instead of just caricaturing their positions. Only by trying to understand them will we be able to work and worship in harmony, even if we still disagree.

For reasons of space we have selected only three issues that we considered important. You may have selected a different three from the list of thirty or three hundred that we could have drawn up!

Sprinklers and dippers

Does your church have a font or a baptistry?

Most Christians would agree that baptism in an important symbol of the grace of God. It looks backwards or forwards

- to a time of new spiritual birth;
- to a cleansing from sin;
- to a dying to one's old self;
- to a resurrection to new life in Christ;
- to becoming a member of God's family.

Before going any further we need to clarify some labels. 'Paedobaptist' describes those who practise infant baptism, usually by wetting the forehead, such as Anglicans, Roman Catholics, and Methodists. They get their label from *pais*, the Greek word for 'child'. Although paedobaptists occasionally baptize believing adults, the majority of baptisms they conduct are of babies who are too young to have expressed faith. 'Baptist' describes those who baptize believing adults, usually by total immersion, such as Baptists, Pentecostals, and most house churches. Baptists will occasionally baptize children if the church leaders are satisfied that the child is a genuine believer.

Some sections of the church believe that baptism isn't just a symbol of God's grace, but, in some mysterious way, is actually effective as a means of grace, regardless of faith on

48

the part of the recipient. This view became popular in the second century. Church Fathers, such as Augustine, taught that unbaptized children are lost for eternity. Many non-churchgoers appear to hold a similar view. They want to have the baby 'done' just in case 'anything should happen' to it.

Evangelical paedobaptists would feel unhappy with such a position but would still remain committed to baptizing infants. In the case of a child from a non-Christian family, they would point to the beneficial effects likely to follow the contact between the child, the family, and the church. Who can measure the effectiveness of the prayers of the church and the family for the child?

When baptizing a child from a Christian family they would argue that they have very strong support. Since the Reformation the main paedobaptist argument in such cases is their belief that baptism is the New Testament equivalent of Old Testament circumcision.

At the risk of over-simplification, the *paedobaptist* argument goes something like this:

> *In the Old Testament, God established a covenant with his people. He required all male babies to be circumcised as a sign that the Jews were a separate people and that God had called them to be his own.*
>
> *Like the new covenant, the covenant made with Abraham was primarily a spiritual one and is always interpreted in the New Testament as such (Romans 4:16–18; 2 Corinthians 6:16–18). It is also clear that, like baptism, circumcision had spiritual significance (Deuteronomy 10:16; 30:6). Baptism has replaced circumcision as the sign and seal of the covenant, and just as male Jewish babies were circumcised, all babies of believers should be baptized.*
>
> *At a later age, all the children individually would be expected to express their own faith (encouraged by the faith*

49

*and prayers of their family) by becoming holy followers of
God. Clearly, not everybody in Israel responded to God's
grace. Nevertheless, the act of circumcision was a clear sign
that this child was part of God's people, a testimony to God's
grace, and a reminder to be separate and holy.*

*The children of believers are baptized, not because it is
assumed that they will become believers themselves, but as a
testimony to God's covenant.*

Paedobaptists accept that in the New Testament baptism appears to follow saving faith. They argue, however, that the adults who were baptized in the New Testament were the first generation of the new covenant. They received its sign as adults, having grown up under the old covenant. It was impossible for them to have been baptized as children.

Baptists stress both the differences between the old and new covenants, and the need for saving faith by the person baptized. They say that the old covenant involved setting up a physical as well as a spiritual kingdom. Even if all Jews were not the spiritual heirs of Abraham, they did live in the land promised to him. Circumcision was partially a sign of race and religion as well as of spirituality. All Jewish males were circumcised because they were physically part of a special people. The new covenant, however, is different. It is entered only by spiritual birth (John 3:1–21). They support their argument from passages in Acts which describe the practice of the early church. People were converted and *then* baptized (Acts 2:38–41; 8:34–39; 9:17–19; 10:44–48; 16:29–34).

Baptists also claim that the original word for 'baptize' strongly implies total immersion as it was used of people being drowned and of ships being sunk. Total immersion is an important symbol, not only of thorough cleansing, but also of death to self (going down into the water) and of resurrection to new life in Christ (coming out of the water; see Romans 6:2–6).

If baptism is to be a means of grace, baptists maintain that it isn't because it's mysterious, but because of the understanding and faith of the recipients. Noah's descendants were blessed when they saw the rainbow only if they understood what it meant and believed what God had said. According to baptists, those who are baptized are strengthened spiritually as they remind themselves of the meaning of the symbol of how God's grace has changed their lives.

We, James and Nina, know of one church where they baptize babies and believing adults by sprinkling, or believing adults by total immersion. Many churches don't make a particular type of baptism a condition for full participation in church life. They are determined not to allow baptism to become a reason for separation. As we try to walk as new creatures in Christ, let's make sure that our old self (of whose death baptism reminds us!) doesn't cause unnecessary division.

Preachers and prophets

We were at a large Christian gathering. A minister came to the microphone and said he believed God had given him a picture to share with us. He described his picture and what he thought God was saying. We listened and evaluated what he said. A few minutes later he preached a standard twenty-minute sermon. We listened and evaluated what he said.

How does God communicate in your church? For many Christians he communicates through sermons and Bible studies which have been prepared by the preacher. Other Christians acknowledge that he speaks through sermons, but claim that he also speaks in a variety of other ways; through prophecy, tongues and interpretation, and through visions.

Christians on both sides of this barricade have libraries full of juicy horror stories that they could tell against each other, but such material is no ground for deciding doctrine. The crucial difference concerns whether or not certain events which are described in the Bible are meant to be taken as normative for today. Should we expect people to experience the Holy Spirit coming on them in a dramatic way? Should we expect people to prophesy? Should we expect people to perform miracles, or speak in tongues? For charismatics the answer to these questions is so obviously 'Yes' that there is a strong temptation to dismiss non-charismatics proudly and not listen to what they are saying.

Non-charismatics argue that charismatics are following the Bible too simply. The main non-charismatic case is that key passages have been misused naïvely to teach something which God never intended. At the risk of over-simplifying their position, the argument goes something like this:

> *When the Holy Spirit was given to the church in Acts 2, he came in a dramatic way. There are similar outpourings of the Holy Spirit accompanied by signs in Acts 8 and 10.*
> *We should not argue from these passages that believers are converted first, and that they should then be 'baptized in the Spirit' – a dramatic experience during which they should speak in tongues. The Holy Spirit was given in a dramatic way in Acts 2 as a clear sign that the Holy Spirit had come. It was a unique occasion at the beginning of a new spiritual era. The occasions in Acts 8 and 10 should be seen in the same light. God was showing the young Jewish church that missionary work to the Gentiles and Samaritans was valid by giving his Spirit to these groups in such a clear way. They, too, were part of the new kingdom.*

Non-charismatics point out that miracles appear in clusters in the Bible and are not uniformly spread throughout history. God appears to choose to do special things at certain times. The birth of the new church was clearly one such time, but miracles and prophecies should not be taken as the norm for all ages and for all churches. 'But where there are prophecies, they will cease ... when perfection comes, the imperfect disappears,' says Paul (1 Corinthians 13:8, 10). Some interpret this to mean that all so-called 'spiritual gifts' ceased after the time of the apostles, now that God's revelation is complete.

On the other hand, *charismatics* argue that in 1 Corinthians 13 Paul is talking about the end of the world, and that you can't prove the cessation of charismatic gifts at the end of the first century from this text. They draw attention to passages from the Old as well as the New Testament to show that God's Spirit came on people in dramatic ways (for example, Judges 6:34; 11:29; 1 Samuel 10:6; 11:6).

One of their key verses is the promise in Joel 2:28–29: 'I will pour out my Spirit on all people. Your sons and daughters will prophesy, your old men will dream dreams, your young men will see visions. Even on my servants, both men and women, I will pour out my Spirit in those days.' From this they argue that the Spirit is no longer limited to certain people and that all believers can enjoy some of the supernatural gifts described in the New Testament.

The Christian who says: 'Three things remain: faith, hope, and speaking in tongues,'[2] clearly has a faulty biblical understanding, and many charismatics have harmed their case when they have placed undue emphasis on 'supernatural gifts'. But the Christian who says: 'Three things abide: a hymn sandwich, notices, and a forty-minute sermon (with one man doing all of the talking all of the time)' is also failing to reflect biblical practices. Many non-charismatics have harmed their case by seeming to want a one-man, non-supernatural religion. There have been, and still are, faults and abuses on both sides.

As you try to work out your own thinking on this topic, don't lose sight of real spirituality. This is judged, not just by what we do, or don't do, but also by our attitude of love towards our brothers and sisters. If you are tempted to storm out of a prayer meeting because the person sitting next to you is continually 'whispering' in tongues, or if you are tempted to leave a church because there is no opportunity to share your prophecy, remember the essential unity you have with these people. Let's get our position on 'charismatic gifts' into a biblical perspective and work to maintain love.

Women and men

About twenty years ago you could go to an evangelistic meeting with secondary-school students and guarantee that at least one bright spark would ask: 'Is God an astronaut?' (The writings of Erich Von Daniken, who claimed that God was a visitor from outer space, were popular at the time.) Before you laugh too much, you should be aware that theological tomes are being written today about what some would see as an equally strange question: 'Is God a man or a woman?' For ordinary church members the issue finds expression in a range of questions such as:

- Should there be women preachers?
- Should women become priests, deacons, elders, or bishops?
- Should women administer baptism and communion?

When considering the other topics in this chapter it has been relatively easy to characterize both sides of the divide. But there are at least three separate arguments to consider when trying to understand why some Christians would assign different roles to women and men in churches. As we think about the issues individually for ease of reference, bear in mind that, for many Christians, two if not all three of the strands are twisted into a strong argument.

Priesthood

For Christians from the Roman Catholic or Anglo-Catholic traditions, the issue centres on what they understand by the priesthood. Great emphasis is placed on the ceremonial, or the visual drama of the services, and on God's representative standing before the altar with the sacrifices of the people. It is argued that as God chose to reveal himself as a man, his representative in church, ministering God's grace through the sacraments and the preaching of the Word, should also be male. It is also argued that because Jesus deliberately chose twelve male apostles, only their male successors (bishops) may ordain priests, and these priests must be male. Although there are women prophets in the Bible, there are no female priests.

Headship

Other Christians, mainly from the Reformed tradition, reject this notion of the priesthood. They argue that in the New Testament all Christians are priests (1 Peter 2:5, 9) and the term is never applied to a restricted group of Christians, or to a particular office in the church. For them, the issue of women priests is a non-starter because they don't accept that there should be priests anyway.

Nevertheless, they would be unhappy with women in church leadership (as a minister, elder, or pastor) for a different reason. They argue from verses such as 1 Corinthians 11:3, Ephesians 5:22–24, and 1 Timothy 2:12 that the New Testament teaches that men are to have 'spiritual authority' over women. Women are not inferior; it is just that God has assigned a different role to them, in the same way that God the Son has a different role from that of God the Father.

A few churches which take this line would be willing to have women preachers and teachers, working as part of a ministry team, under the authority of a male leader.

Male teachers

A third strand in the argument concerns the verses in the New Testament which seem to say that women should not teach men. Paul writes: 'I do not permit a woman to teach or have authority over a man; she must be silent' (1 Timothy 2:12); 'Women should remain silent in the churches. They are not allowed to speak' (1 Corinthians 14:34). In some churches this 'silence' appears to mean they can give talks to children and ladies' groups, but they are not allowed to teach where adult males will be present.

Wrestling with unease

The issue can be a painful one. Women are continually reminded that the church is male-dominated, even if well over 50% of the congregation is female. The presence of women is hidden when they find themselves singing lines such as 'Rise up, O men of God', or 'Now I am your son, I am adopted in your family . . .'.

On occasions their spiritual gifts have to remain hidden while they watch some ungifted men mishandling administration or pastoral situations, and preaching superficial sermons. Some women (and men) are passionately concerned about the image of Christianity that is being communicated to the world. They are embarrassed that their female friends and daughters are being expected to become part of a family where women seem second-class.

Those who are unhappy with the teaching about the case for male priests, elders and teachers have responded in one of three ways. First, some have rejected the Bible as authoritative, arguing that it promotes an oppressive patriarchal structure. Secondly, some have taken their teaching from their experience, rather than from the Bible. They argue that missionary work would have been seriously hindered without women teachers, that they have been spiritually taught by Christian books from women writers, and that they have been helped by some excellent women speakers. They wouldn't say that 1 Timothy 2:12 is wrong; they would just prefer not to think about it.

A third response has come from those who wish to remain in submission to the teaching of the Bible. They have sought to show that the biblical material is more complex than is often admitted. They have found support from their understanding of the human side of the Bible (see chapter 4).

This last group argue that although much of the biblical imagery of God is male, female imagery does exist. God is described as a mother (Isaiah 49:13–15; 66:13), a pregnant woman (Isaiah 42:14), a midwife (Psalm 22:9), a seamstress (Genesis 3:21).

They argue that it is difficult to see how the so-called 'silence texts' prohibit women from teaching and making spiritual judgments affecting men when other passages are taken into account. Joel had predicted that sons *and daughters* would prophesy (Joel 2:28–29), and clearly, female prophets existed (Exodus 15:20; Judges 4:4; 2 Kings 22:14; Nehemiah 6:14; Isaiah 8:3; Luke 2:36; Acts 21:9). There was also a female judge (Judges 4:4), and Junia, an apostle (Romans 16:7).[3] Priscilla was involved in teaching Apollos (Acts 18:26). 1 Corinthians 14:34 seems to be in conflict with verse 29 in the same chapter, where the whole church is called on to evaluate the prophets, and with 1 Corinthians 11:2–16 where Paul is condemning uncovered female heads during prophecy, not women prophets. In 1 Corinthians 14 the issue is more likely to be to do with chattering and interruption than with teaching. In 2 Timothy 2:2 ('The things you have heard me say in the presence of many witnesses entrust to reliable men who will also be qualified to teach others'), the word translated 'men' really means 'people'.

The second line of argument used by this group is that

the seemingly negative verses about women have to be interpreted in the light of the culture to which they were written. The absence of priestesses in the Old Testament may be explained by a desire to avoid the dangers of the fertility cults and sacred prostitution that were so common in the enemies of Israel. In an age when women had little education, it is easy to see why they wouldn't necessarily make the best teachers, and why Paul exhorts them to 'learn in quietness' (1 Timothy 2:11). Given that some rabbis thought teaching the law to daughters was as useful as burning it, Paul's encouragement to women to learn was itself quite revolutionary. Equally, Paul's advice to Timothy is not surprising when seen against the female-based fertility cults which threatened the early church (Revelation 2:20; 2 Peter 2:14–15; 2 Timothy 3:6–7). Michael Green argues[4] that the word translated 'have authority over' in 1 Timothy 2:12 has strong sexual overtones. He suggests that St John Chrysostom may have been right in interpreting Paul as saying he does not allow women to teach men obscenity and fornication. Although men must share the blame for sexual sin, this advice is particularly appropriate for churches in cities where religious prostitution was common.

A third line of argument used by these Christians is that there are practices in the Bible which were part of the culture of the time, but which were never part of God's original plan for people. God regulated polygamy and divorce without either of them being part of his divine intent. Paul accepted slavery without necessarily condoning it. Male domination existed in the cultures in which the Bible was written. It is argued that such masculine pre-eminence is not the intent of the God who chose women as the first witnesses to the resurrection, and who gave his Son to break down barriers between Jew and Gentile, slave and free, male and female (Galatians 3:28).

Remember that any views you hold at the moment are bound to have been influenced by your experiences – whether you are female or male, single or married, leader or led, teacher or taught – and by your present church background. As you seek to examine your own position on this matter, prayerfully take a fresh look at the biblical passages. If you consider all the material, it becomes a complex issue and you are unlikely to reach any clear conclusion overnight.

Weighing up the relative importance

So far in this chapter we have been focusing on differences between Christians. Although these differences are important, we don't want to lose sight of the fact that all Christians have many things in common. We share a belief that salvation comes in response to the grace of God. We are forgiven because of Christ's death. We have hope because of his resurrection. We share a belief that God is committed to building his church and that he has chosen to do this mainly through the obedience of individual Christians. We are united in wanting to see repentance, worship, fellowship, teaching, evangelism and social action as being part of any normal Christian life. The importance of any differences we may have has to be judged against this background.

Suppose the only church in your village is a paedobaptist one, but you are a convinced baptist. Should you make the twenty-mile round trip twice on a Sunday to go to the nearest Baptist church, or should you throw your lot in with the local Methodists?

We can't answer that one for you, but we would ask you to evaluate the importance of baptism as an issue. We think it would be wrong for you to make that decision on the basis of a church's teaching on baptism alone. You would have to take other issues into account. And matters such as a belief in the authority of the Bible, and a commitment to evangelism and service, are much more important than a particular view of liturgical practice. For example, does either church have leaders who believe the Bible to be the inspired Word of God and who are striving to teach it well? If the answer is 'No' for one and 'Yes' for the other, you would, in the long term, be better off going to the church that gives you biblical teaching, regardless of its views on baptism.

Suppose you believe that you have the gift of tongues and of prophecy and attend an independent evangelical church where the minister is opposed to 'charismatic gifts'. You know that there is no opportunity in your church services to exercise the gifts, and that 98% of the congregation would have kittens or heart attacks if you did. The Anglo-Catholic church down the road has recently 'gone charismatic', but you're not sure if you could cope with the candles, and you feel you might miss the ministry and ache for the active evangelism that you have enjoyed at your present church. What should you do?

Again, we can't answer that one for you, but we would ask you to evaluate the importance of charismatic gifts as an issue. We think it would be wrong for you to make that decision on the basis of a church's teaching on these gifts alone. You need to ask yourself if the new church would provide you with essential teaching and opportunities for service, as well as allowing you to express your gifts. In addition to considering the cost to yourself, you would also need to consider the cost to your present church of your leaving. You shouldn't make charismatic gifts the only issue. There are bigger things to consider.

If you decided to stay you could still use your 'charismatic gifts' in a subtle way. Tongues are given for individual building up and don't have to be prayed in church. You can still pray in tongues at home and in English at church. And you can still express your prophecies in other ways, either by sharing in prayer-times what you believe God has put into your heart, or by discussing what you believe God is saying with individuals and with the church leaders.

The relative importance of all of the topics discussed in this chapter need to be evaluated in a similar way. We will return to this topic when we consider whether and when it is right to leave a church (in chapters 11 and 12).

Handling differences

At the end of the last chapter we offered three tips for handling differences (accept your brothers and sisters; don't be simplistic or lazy; see elephants as elephants and nits as nits). Here are five more tips. Many of our friends, family, and fellow church members will recognize that we have learned some of them by our mistakes.

Don't be surprised

Differences will always exist because of God's created variety, or because of our sin.

Have big anchors

It's easy to run away, and most of us depart too readily. It's more biblical, painful, and helpful to stay and work through issues. If you run away physically (by leaving the church), or if you run away emotionally and intellectually (by clamming up, avoiding real communication with the people, and pretending that the difference doesn't exist) you are helping Satan do his work of division, and you are missing an opportunity for real Christian growth. We have to learn to talk through differences. Running, if it happens at all, should be a last, not a first, resort.

Hold truth humbly

Don't make the mistake of thinking that your sinful mind is perfect and that those who differ from you are *always* wrong.

Don't become unteachable by thinking you have nothing to learn. Even students, church leaders, Sunday School superintendents, and people who've been Christians for decades need to learn new things!

Grow big ears

Most communication experts agree that we don't listen enough to what people are actually saying. We take in a few words, then *guess* what they are saying (in the light of our fears and prejudices) and start to plan a reply. Consequently, we often get it wrong. An Anglican charismatic might ask for more songs to be put together in one place in the service to help a time of worship. You might interpret this as an attempt to abandon the liturgy and limit the time available for preaching. But it might just be a request for more singing to be put together in one place in the service to create an uninterrupted time of worship.

Cultivate a big heart

Be sensitive to others and let Christian love limit your freedom. Let God worry about whether those who are different are right or wrong. You must take responsibility for your own reaction to them and strive, as far as possible, to guard the relationship. If you are a leader and have to do something which is right rather than popular, act with humility rather than arrogance. Do these things and people may eventually listen to your case; if you don't, you'll never stand a chance of getting a real hearing.

In looking at these issues we have been considering problems which mainly show themselves as theological differences. They can often appear as doctrinal divisions in the large body of Christ in any town or city. Most of the difficulties in coping with our own congregation, however, aren't usually to do with theology. It could be argued that most church problems are not really to do with doctrine, but with human relationships. We often have difficulty in coping with our local church because of a failure to be spiritual. It's to this topic that we now turn.

CHAPTER 6

SPIRITUAL FAILURE

In the previous two chapters we have considered differences of belief. Another cause of pain amongst Christians is our inability to consistently relate well to other family members. We don't always handle conflict in a biblical way. And sometimes an apparent doctrinal difference is just a cover-up for a more mundane problem over a relationship. If somebody has hurt us, we are more likely to reject his views on tithing or disagree with her over proposed changes to the church worship.

An outwardly 'religious' problem was used to disguise a more mundane relationship grievance between Moses, Aaron, and Miriam. At the beginning of Numbers 12 we are told that Miriam and Aaron began to talk against Moses, and initially the reason given for this grumbling is that he had married a Cushite. The crux of the religious objection appears to be either that Moses was marrying a foreign woman, or that he was taking a second wife when Zipporah, his first wife, was not yet dead.

What is interesting is that the Holy Spirit doesn't

comment on the rightness of their accusation against Moses. God does, however, reveal Miriam's and Aaron's *real motive* for complaining and takes them to task for it. 'Has the Lord spoken only through Moses?' they asked. 'Hasn't he also spoken through us?' (Numbers 12:2).

They certainly had been used by God. Aaron was the mouthpiece for the frightened Moses. He had seen all that had happened in the Egyptian court as a result of the God-given words which he spoke. In Exodus 15:20–21 we can also read of Miriam's service. She was one of the first charismatics – tambourines, dancing, singing a chorus, prophecy. And yet Miriam and Aaron had become proud, and felt threatened by what God was doing through Moses. Their jealousy stands in contrast to Moses' humility. Their accusation against Moses had become a religious cover for a sinful way of relating.

Problem people

Some people are very difficult to live with. Most churches have at least one of the following people in them. See if you can recognize yourself.

The Prima Donnas

The touchy ones who think they can dominate the whole show.

I have been in our church for years. Because I have been a large fish in a small pond which has been undisturbed for some time (the leader of the small Sunday School and the person in charge of the cleaning rota) I think that the spotlight should always shine on me. I have an inexhaustible supply of wisdom on all topics under the sun, and should always be consulted about everything. I take offence easily if I am not given the respect my status deserves. I like to keep newcomers in their place. I sulk easily if things are changed in a way which is inconvenient for me. I often resort to threats in an attempt to get my own way.

The Lone Rangers

The people who think it is smart to ride alone.

As a lone ranger I rarely go to meetings these days. I prefer to keep myself to myself. I used to go at one time. But then things started going down hill in the church. I started being late to meetings. I always tried to sit 'outside the group' if I could, or I sat at the back so that I could watch the others. Now I can no longer identify with the church. I just let them get on with it. I always refuse invitations to people's homes. I have convinced myself that isolation is always a true mark of spirituality. I still try to worship by myself. Who needs people when you can get good ministry from a cassette player?

The Jugs of Custard

The people who get upset over trifles.

You'll never guess what happened this morning. The minister forgot to announce the total for last week's collection. I had spent at least fifteen minutes checking the total for him and writing it out. Some people said it was a fantastic service. Apparently he led the worship with great sensitivity and the sermon was powerful, illuminating, challenging, and encouraging. But I missed all that because I was so angry about his incompetence over the notices. I'm going to tell him about it just before the evening service.

The Peacocks

The people who think they are wonderful and like everyone to know it.

I'm an amazing youth leader, always having great ideas to

improve my already brilliant sessions. I get up at 6 a.m. for a two-hour quiet time which makes me feel spiritual for the whole day. I always make a lot of prayer requests at meetings (just in case you should forget how important my service is). My own prayers are usually answered ('the prayers of a righteous person . . .' and all that). I honestly can't understand your difficulty. I've led sixteen people to Christ already this year . . .

If space permitted we could go on to describe

- the Nostalgia Junkies (those people who hide in the past so that they don't have to face the present);
- the Placaters (those unhappy people who say 'Yes' to everybody and everything just for a quiet life);
- the Freezers (those who cope with conflict by freezing out those they disagree with);
- the Outlaws (those who are convinced that the rules don't apply to them);
- the Shoppers (those who move from church to church looking for the best bargain at the least cost);
- the Gas Rings (those who cope with conflict by bursting into flame at the slightest spark and scorch others);
- the Pharisees (those who think that spirituality is defined in terms of obeying 257 'Don'ts' a day).

We're sure you could add plenty of other character types to our list.

Spiritual failure causes much heartache and grieves God. It usually shows itself in resistance to change and in poor relationships. And yet it is through changing, and through loving unlovely people, that most churches grow. In the next chapter we will explore the subject of change in church life more fully. In the remainder of this chapter we want to analyse spiritual failure further, and offer practical suggestions for coping with it.

Don't blame the church for what it can't do

Dr Lawrence Crabb, a Christian psychologist, has argued that all people have two very basic needs:[1]

- The need to feel significant.
- The need to feel secure.

When either of those needs is not met, we suffer acute stress and look around for somebody or something to meet our need.

Dr Crabb goes on to say that for the Christian, both of those needs can be met in Jesus. Christ's unconditional love for us gives us security for eternity. We know that nothing can separate us from his love. We also know that in serving him, we have true significance. What could be more honouring than being ambassadors for the Most High God?

For many of us, however, the problem is that we haven't yet *learned* that we have significance and security in Christ. When our human significance or security is hurt, we respond in a human way. If our views are ignored, we strive to get them accepted. We act as if our worth as people depends on their being heard and we forget that God's approval of them is what matters. If we feel threatened by others, we fight back, forgetting that we don't have to prove anything to the one who accepts us and still uses us. We get depressed. We lash out. We strive to gain the things which others depend on for importance. We are unwilling to stand in silence beneath God's loving smile and we want to shout our protests about other people, hoping that we can make a few humans grin at us.

There are times when all of us look to the *church*, and not to *Christ*, to provide us with significance and security. And consequently, when the fallible church inevitably fails to meet those needs, we become hurt and angry, and start blaming individuals and whole congregations.

Rosemary is in her forties and has become very bitter. She rarely makes it to church these days. Her husband John is suffering from the final stages of multiple sclerosis. Rosemary has 'lost' her husband, and feels that she has 'lost' her church because they are unable to adequately meet her need to feel secure in love. Until the 'apathetic many' are prepared to help the 'overworked few' and share in showing practical family love to Rosemary, she will never receive the attention she needs. But even then, it will leave her feeling disappointed.

While her church has a very real responsibility to demonstrate the compassion of Christ to Rosemary in a practical way, Rosemary has to learn to depend for her security on the love of Christ, and not on an imperfect church.

Richard was twenty-two when he moved into the city. He came to the area to marry a daughter of one of the deacons and take up a post as a civil servant. He always wore a suit, and the inside of his new car was usually as meticulously clean as the outside. He was clearly going places! Unfortunately the elders didn't appear to recognize Richard's worth. He was never asked to lead services or preach, despite his having done so in his previous church. Richard's in-laws asked the pastor why Richard hadn't yet been let near the pulpit. He replied that he was waiting to see more signs of spiritual maturity in Richard before he let him loose on the congregation. Richard and his family took the hump for a long time.

Clearly any church has a responsibility to recognize and use people to the glory of God. But Richard has to learn that his significance as a person hinges on his relationship to Christ, and not what he does or doesn't do in the church.

Until we learn to stop looking to the church to meet all our needs, and start finding our fulfilment and peace in Christ, we will always be dissatisfied.

Humility and love

There is a joke, attributed to Gerald Coates, which has a painful element of truth in it: 'Resist the devil and he will flee from you. Resist the deacons and they will fly at you.'

And it's not just the deacons or the PCC who do all the flying either, is it? All of us are capable of counter-attacking when we feel threatened, of being sinfully stubborn when we are out-voted or ignored, and of using spiritual language to cover up basic human jealousy. Such behaviour stems from pride and immature love.

Some people at St Augusta's still talk about the 'curtain dispute' with pain, even though it happened years ago. Neither the vicar nor the churchwardens had the time or the gifts to manage all the practical details relating to the new church hall. The PCC set up a committee of five wise men and women with practical and artistic skills to select and purchase the necessary furniture and fittings.

Within two days of the first meeting of this sub-committee, the vicar had a major dispute on his hands. A wife of one of the members had learned what colour and type of curtains the sub-committee had agreed on. She was so dismayed at the choice that she phoned round and gathered support for her views. The church polarized into two groups. The woman and her supporters eventually got their own way, but they went about it in such a manner as to leave a stream of hurt behind them.

Regardless of the rights or wrongs of the particular case, both sides 'lost' when they started to approach the matter as if they had to 'win' at all costs.

Pride and lovelessness show themselves in our churches in many forms – in failure to submit to the leadership and to one another, in jealousy and anger, in bitterness, in a failure to forgive. The way to defeat these things is to respond, not how we naturally want to, but as

Christ would have done, through his Spirit who indwells us (Ephesians 4:29–32). Any version of spirituality which does not arise from the Holy Spirit simply cannot be holy.

Maintain good relations, despite disagreements

In Matthew 7:1 Jesus tells us not to judge other people. In Philippians 2:3 Paul tells us to think of others as better than ourselves. Does this mean that we have to suspend all our critical faculties? Should we be afraid of thinking that someone's obvious sinful behaviour is wrong? If God has given us a clear gift of administration that has been recognized by others for years, do we have to pretend that a manifestly incompetent administrator is doing a better job than we would have done?

These verses aren't commanding us to suspend all critical judgment in relation to other people. For one thing, we have been made in God's image with the ability to distinguish between good and evil, even between good and better. The Bible also encourages us to use our powers of judgment. If we are to avoid throwing pearls to swine, we have to be able to recognize swine as swine![2]

While these verses do not ask us to suspend our judgment, they do warn us against the danger of being over-critical in our judgment. For example, I may legitimately think that a church committee made the wrong decision about how to introduce changes in missionary support, and I may also feel that its members introduced those changes in the wrong way. This difference of judgment, however, gives me no right to attempt to hurt or destroy the people involved by gossiping about them, by withdrawing fellowship from them, by automatically resisting all other plans they may have, and by completely failing to see God's grace in their lives.

You can just imagine the conversation between some

Pharisees after Jesus had disturbed their spiritual sleep: 'I mean, I know he walked on water, calmed storms, made the blind see, and raised Lazarus from the dead, but you can't trust a word he says because he eats with tax collectors and immoral people!'

There's a world of difference between the gentle and compassionate criticism of someone who loves you and who genuinely wants to help you, and the negative response of someone who wants to cut you down to size, or who is jealous of you. Lovelessness and pride are harsh and destructive. They speak out of fear or jealousy. They want to push people away, not hold on to them.

Don't let your judgment about issues destroy relationships with your church family. You don't have to abandon your views, but you must learn to think and talk positively about people who oppose you, and about what God is doing in them. Pray for your enemies in your own church family (Matthew 5:44).

Joyce Huggett has described[3] the radical change that came about in one congregation when she asked its warring members to write down some positive things about each other. It helped them to see some light shining through their sinful thinking about their church family. Make a list of the positive qualities of your opponents. Surprise yourself and others by writing letters of apology. We can confess the sinful thoughts and words about others that we have encouraged, and we can be free to let God evaluate the justice of our cause. We cannot be held responsible for the sin of others, but we must take full responsibility for our own sinful reactions to them.

Hold Christ firmly

We have every right to expect the body of Christ to minister to its members. As has been argued above, however, we shouldn't expect the church to meet all our needs for security and significance. The church is not the perfect kingdom of God, and sinful Christians may fail to provide the security and recognition that we need.

When the church hurts us, God wants to use that pain to drive us closer to himself. Although churches should help us in our discipleship, there may well be times when we have to cling to Christ despite the church. During such times, run to Christ for comfort. Spend more time alone with him in worship and prayer. Pour out your heart to him. Tell him about the injustice that you feel and about the consequences you fear. Cry to him for the Holy Spirit as you struggle to love your enemies. It grieves us that we are unrecognized, but God alone can say the 'Well done' that has any lasting value. We want people to like us, but it is the love of Christ alone which provides ultimate security.

Become an enthusiastic servant

You can imagine the petty differences and jealousies that must have existed between the disciples. Differences in personality, background, and persuasion made an 'interesting' mix. A Jewish Zealot found himself working with a converted tax-collector who had served the Romans. The nine left behind to fail in the valley wondered for months why Jesus took the three on to the mountain to witness his transfiguration (Mark 9:2–32). And there were arguments about who would have what position when Jesus came into his kingdom (Mark 9:33–34; 10:35–37). Judas Iscariot was beginning to distance himself from the rest.

It had been a long, tiring day, and they found themselves in a room with dust on their feet. But they all had their position to think of. Why should they do the dirty work for these other ungrateful, and sometimes objectionable, people?

And then Jesus rolled up his sleeves and washed their feet (John 13:1–17). Humility and mature love are prepared

73

to put self aside in order to become a servant. Pride and lovelessness cling on to status and rights.

The people who are most free are those who have nothing to lose. Jesus had that freedom because he had already laid aside everything by choosing to go to the cross. Even his most precious 'possession', his relationship with the Father, was soon to be mysteriously and temporarily broken as he took our sin on himself and was punished. If we have chosen to be crucified with Christ, and are seeking daily to die to self, then we become free to serve. We have nothing else to lose. We can choose to put self aside, and serve unconditionally.

The trouble with a living sacrifice is that it keeps crawling off the altar.[4]

Yes, you know that your real gift is in music, and you resent being left with the job of counting the collection and cleaning the building because everybody else is on holiday, ill, or unwilling. And given that the minister has less than tactfully pointed out that you play too slowly, the congregation has criticized you for playing too fast, and the young people have dropped heavy hints about their desire to replace your subtle arrangements with an electric guitar and a set of drums, you have more than once wanted to leave the church. But, once you remind yourself that you have been forgiven by God and granted the privilege of serving him, and once you realize that he understands and evaluates everything, you find yourself singing a chorus as you scrub the church toilets!

Paul urges us to 'overcome evil with good' (Romans 12:21). The greatest in the kingdom of God are those who serve (Mark 9:35). Even the Son of Man did not come to be served, but to serve (Mark 10:45).

Decide to love

Most of us can recognize immature love. It is the kind of love that can't cope with difference or failure. It says: 'I will love you *if* you do this or that. My love for you is conditional on your good behaviour, or your agreement with me.'

When practised in marriage, immature love leaves one partner desperately trying to earn the other's affection, and becoming bitter as she or he fails. When immature parents adopt such attitudes to their children it results in terribly insecure children who eventually resent playing the game of trying to win mummy's or daddy's love. We're saddened by unhealthy family relationships. We instinctively want to help such people to understand that mature love isn't just a feeling, but a decision to behave positively towards others and to act for their benefit unconditionally.

The tragedy is that although Jesus demonstrated such unconditional love towards his followers and commanded them to show such love towards one another, many churches display cold or antagonistic relationships between members and towards other churches. We so easily slip into the habit of playing the conditional-love game:

'I will speak to her *if* she speaks to me.'

'I will invite them round for a meal *if* they invite me.'

'I will play ball with him *if* he plays ball with me!'

God continued to work for Abraham after he lied, for Moses after he murdered, for David after he committed adultery, for Peter after he denied Jesus, and for Paul after his hurtful dispute with Barnabas. Sadly, many of us would have whispered about these people and cold-shouldered them for years. The power of spiritual failure in churches can be broken only when we are prepared to choose to be humble, and to choose to show mature love.

'I do not leave you alone'

Many of us like to wrestle. Unfortunately, we often insist on wrestling against flesh and blood, and not against the spiritual

75

powers of darkness in the heavenly places (Ephesians 6:12). Sometimes the 'flesh and blood' is so overpowering that we lose sight of the spiritual dimension. In fact, the people concerned may dominate our thinking so much that we find it difficult to pray. We feel like the minister who fell into a bitter dispute with his church and was asked to leave. Before taking up his post as a prison chaplain, he preached his final sermon on John 14:2 (AV): 'I go to prepare a place for you'![5]

We want to close this chapter with an obvious, but necessary, reminder that our only hope of dealing with spiritual failure is for us to become more Christlike as we know more of the Holy Spirit. Being full of the Holy Spirit isn't really about having tingly feelings. It's about consciously choosing to serve, love, and honour those who are gossiping about you, frustrating your plans, wearing you down, and upsetting your friend.

As your heart weeps, cry to God for the Holy Spirit. Remind yourself that the Father sees your pain and is longing to strengthen you. Don't be content with any past changes or experiences. Ask God to give you fresh grace for now. Remind yourself:

- Satan brings the destruction of relationships and plans, but the Holy Spirit brings re-creation and hope.
- Satan brings pain and crushed spirits, but the Holy Spirit brings healing and open hearts.
- Satan brings bitterness and emptiness, but the Holy Spirit brings joy and fulness.
- Satan brings jealousy and bondage, but the Holy Spirit brings contentment and freedom.
- Satan brings rudeness and pride, but the Holy Spirit brings gentleness and brokenness.
- Satan creates unnecessary barriers, but the Holy Spirit strives for unity.
- Satan brings problems, but the Holy Spirit facilitates solutions.

Pray for the Holy Spirit to act, and seek to honour him by

loving your church. Without him, we and our churches are a lost cause. With him, people are converted, Christians become more like Jesus (full of love, joy, peace, patience, kindness, goodness, faithfulness, gentleness, and self-control; Galatians 5:22–23) and churches change. God is full of mercy and grace. He *can* help us and our churches.

CHAPTER 7

CHANGE OR DECAY?

Changing things in churches is often like eating a crunchy peanut butter sandwich – the lumps get stuck in your teeth, the smooth gets stuck to the top of your mouth, and you feel as if you'll never finish the first round; however, it's usually worth it in the end!

The need for change

Where will your church be in a hundred years' time? Of course, none of us can tell. We can be reasonably sure, however, that unless it changes from what it is now, it will have ceased to exist, or will have become irrelevant to the needs of most people.

Many of us feel uneasy with change, and Satan is able to use this to provoke wars between us. How many major disputes between Christians in the same congregation have been caused over somebody's sincere attempt to introduce what, to any outside observer, may seem a relatively minor change?

Sometimes we try to give spiritual justification for being ostriches by appealing to the unchanging nature of Christ and of basic human need. We argue that society may change, but people still basically need to be forgiven and to enter into a relationship with God. All we have to do is to keep preaching that message and everything will be all right! We forget that God may still have some teaching and changing to do in our lives that will influence the way we worship and evangelize, for example. And we forget that although people's basic needs are the same, the external fabric and tastes of the lives of each generation are different from those of the previous one.

We are not advocating change just for change's sake. We shouldn't repair something unless it's broken and shouldn't break anything unless we can repair it. Congregations that have faced major upheavals and reviews of their procedures often need periods of stability. The rest of recuperation, however, should not become the stillness of death. Let us briefly suggest two reasons why any church may need to change.

Changed context

Sometimes a church ought to change because the needs of the people change. North Puddlethorpe was originally a quiet village and the church attracted a rural congregation. As the nearby town expanded, however, North Puddlethorpe became part of the commuter belt, and house prices rocketed. People who moved into the area tended to be middle-aged 'successful' professionals. Volvos and Saabs were more common than Fords. An evangelistic business lunch in the local pub, with a solicitor presenting the message, was more likely to attract people than a family service aimed at mums and toddlers. And although Joe, the local farmer, could 'preach the gospel', his message wasn't really meeting the needs of the managing director who was struggling with his conscience over a bribe he had given in order to secure a contract, or the headteacher, recently converted, who was trying to reconcile her scientific training with a fundamentalist book she was reading.

A large council estate in the nearby town used to be full of families, and the church there had had a thriving youth work. For reasons which planners couldn't quite understand, however, this estate had become very 'settled'. The original couples had tended to stay put. But their children had now grown up and many had moved away. The school had closed. The church's youth work was dwindling. Unless the church rapidly changed its strategy to minister to the needs of the poor and the elderly, it would become irrelevant to the community and would eventually die.

Numerical or spiritual growth

Growth is a major stimulant to change. What changes would have to take place in your church if revival broke out and your congregation doubled in size?

An increase in size requires changes in *administration*. Churches which start off small go through difficult periods when they see growth. Sometimes the original members want to retain an informal atmosphere and don't want too much organization. Reluctantly, growing churches often have to create order out of chaos. We see the apostles experiencing the need to change in response to growth in Acts 6:1–7, where they selected people to help with the distribution of the poor relief.

When growth happens, it brings *new teaching needs*. For example, a church of twenty-five didn't need to regularly train housegroup leaders, preachers, and counsellors. But when the church grew to 225, training became a key responsibility for the minister. A church that has new converts needs a programme for them, which it doesn't need without them.

Perhaps the most difficult pressure for change is that which comes, not from numerical growth within the church, but from changes in *personal needs* and from personal growth within.

John and Rita recently moved back to the city where they had been students. They had married after graduating, had been away for eighteen years, and now had four children. One of the things they dreaded about the move was finding a new church, because they knew they couldn't return to the one they had enjoyed as students.

They had left the church after three marvellous years there. It was large and 'sound'. But eighteen years later they saw that little had changed, even though *they* had changed considerably. Their expression of worship was different now from what it had been then, and they wanted something good for the children. But there was nothing specifically for the children in the service, and the Sunday School seemed so old-fashioned. They were keen to exercise their own leadership and teaching gifts and didn't see much opportunity in this church. They didn't want to become pew fodder. They just didn't seem to 'fit' here any more.

At the risk of over-simplification, the twentieth century has seen the church rediscover its social conscience and the Holy Spirit. Forty years ago the label 'charismatic' was rarely heard in evangelical circles, and the prospect of ordinary Christians writing to their MPs about a social or moral issue would have seemed extremely strange. Arguably the church, as a whole, has grown in these areas. But growth in the church as a whole happens because *individual Christians* change their thinking and have a new understanding of God.

And whole congregations rarely 'see the light' at the same time. Gradual personal growth represents a constant healthy pressure for change within a single church. Where there's growth, there's life. And where there's life, there's a continual pressure for change. 'To live is to change, and to be perfect is to have changed often' (J. H. Newman).

Have you heard about the boy who swallowed a teaspoon? He hasn't stirred since. Sometimes we seem to forget that repentance and renewal is an on-going process, and that God is continually wanting to shake and stir us. Instead of expecting to be the same in our Christian life from year to year, we ought not only to evaluate change carefully, but to embrace it willingly as a normal part of Christian life. We don't expect a graduation diploma on the first day at school and we shouldn't expect to be made perfect in church after one Sunday. Our earnest prayer ought to be:

Change and decay in all around I see.
And thou who changest not, please, please change me!

Understanding resistance

Sometimes we are so annoyed by people who appear to resist change that we just condemn them. If there is ever to be progress in the healing of relationships or in achieving the desired change, we need to move from initial condemnation to try to understand why these people are resisting. Understanding should help us to be more compassionate and patient. Here are a few reasons why people resist change.

Conservatism

Have you been on holiday more than once in the last five years? If you have, did you go to the same place twice or more, or did you go somewhere different each time?

Some people seek variety and new stimulation more eagerly then others. They have personalities which are more adaptable than others. We know of one couple where the husband is often shocked to return home to a different living room. His wife is easily bored with the arrangement of furniture and frequently tries out something new. Regularity and pattern can help provide all of us with security; but many people genuinely have a lower boredom threshold than others. They find too much regularity a prison. Neither is 'right' or 'wrong'; they're just 'different'. When things need changing, some people find that change much easier than others.

If things are not going well at church, certain people will immediately want to alter the arrangements. Others may find it easier to rationalize the situation and blame God, rather than face the trauma of doing something different. If things are going well, a few people constantly ask: 'How can we do this even better?' Others are content to stay with the 'good' and not worry too much about the 'best'.

Apart from personality, daily experiences may also influence our adaptability. You may work in an environment where you evaluate procedures regularly through discussion with colleagues, change in response to client needs, and continually learn new information and ideas. Your organization or business has to adapt rapidly in order to survive. By contrast, the majority of the people in your church may not encounter such pressures or experiences. They may find change much more unusual and therefore more threatening than you do. We need to understand that people are different.

Vested interests

Some people resist change because they have a vested interest in keeping things as they are.

At Chandelier Baptist Fellowship the leaders were planning a major change in administrative procedures. In response to rapid growth, they had decided to recommend that the church should appoint a full-time administrator equipped with a computer system. This would simplify the accounting and correspondence. It would also improve the quality of church handouts through desktop publishing, and a database of contacts would be established to assist in evangelism and general communication with members.

Up to this point Margaret had served the church well for years as an unpaid secretary to the pastor. As well as her husband, she had a brother and two grown-up children who, with their respective spouses, were all church members. She was not interested in applying for the post, even though the church was willing to send her on a course in new technology.

Nobody was surprised that she, her family, and several close friends opposed the change. It was obviously going to be difficult for Margaret. What surprised everybody was the strength of the opposition and the vehemence of bad feeling that was generated.

Months later, after a communion service, Margaret tried to explain why there had been so much anger. She was honest enough to admit that she felt resentful that she was losing her position of 'special servant to the pastor', with all the status and inside information about what was going on that the job had given her. She was struggling to trust God to provide a different role for her in his body. And this resentment had been inflamed by her family who felt that their own service in the church was being devalued. Because of their number and support, they wanted to think that their position was unassailable.

Genuine fear

Some people oppose change because of fear. Put yourself in the position of the Jerusalem apostles who were confronted by Peter with a story about how a centurion and his household had been converted and received the Holy Spirit, and about how Peter was specifically told by God to enter the Gentile's house (Acts 11). Many of them would have had a genuine fear that in letting the Gentiles in without acceptance of the Jewish ceremonial law, they would in some way be betraying God and watering down his message. I'm sure that at least one of them thought, even if he didn't actually say it: 'Ah, but if you let them get away with not keeping the ceremonial law, it will be the thin end of the wedge, and they'll reject the moral law as well . . . It's the principle of the thing . . .'

Be more sympathetic towards any of your church leaders who may be resisting the changes you want. They have to give an account to God for how they have 'shepherded' the flock that has been entrusted to them. They may fear that the proposed change may not be in the church's best interests.

Fear of admitting past mistakes

The Reverend Michael Jolly was invited to take a weekend retreat for a church where he had been the vicar ten years previously. During his time there, the church had known quite remarkable growth. Over the weekend he tried to share honestly with the people, many of whom had served with him during his ministry there, how God had been graciously changing him since they last were together. He told several stories against himself, laughed at some of the mistakes he thought he had made, and explained how he would approach things differently now.

At the end of the weekend he was cornered by an elderly saint who spoke in an uncharacteristically accusing way: 'So we got it all wrong then . . . all those years.' He had realized that to accept what Michael was now saying would be to imply that they had been doing things wrongly during an important time of growth for the church. The preciousness of the man's memories was being challenged.

Sometimes we do have to face the pain of admitting that we did get it wrong, and that our opposition, words or behaviour were not honouring to God. Often, however, it isn't so straightforward. Michael pointed out that at the time they were following God as best they knew how, and God had honoured that. They had been faithful to the light they had at the time. But now the vicar had moved on in his understanding. To obey God now would mean doing things differently.

Sin

Let's not be blind to the fact that sometimes opposition to change is sinful. And whether or not Satan uses our personality, our fears, our difficulties, or whatever, if we are opposing the change that God wants to bring in our lives and in the life of our church, we are grieving God.

So how can we overcome these obstacles and work to bring about the changes we feel our church needs to make? This is the question we tackle in the next chapter.

CHAPTER *8*

ENCOURAGING CHANGE

This book is not primarily aimed at church leaders. We are therefore not going to address specifically the problems which leaders face in bringing about necessary change (although we hope our more general advice may be helpful to them). You may be an 'ordinary' member of the body who is aware that something is not right, who has a genuine desire to make something better, and who may be struggling with a need for change. What we want to do in this chapter is to offer practical advice on how to encourage change. This is not because we think that all change is automatically 'right'; it's just that there seem to be many people who are frustrated with their present situation and who don't know what to do.

If, on the other hand, your problem is that you are facing change that is making you feel very unhappy, we hope that what we have to say will help you too. Take each one of the principles for encouraging change listed below, and apply it to your situation. For example, you need to be humble when suggesting change, and you also need to be humble when opposing change.

Identify motives

Before we approach anyone with our ideas for change, we need to spend quality time alone with God. We need to ask him to search our heart so that we can try to understand our motives. Let's be honest enough to admit that although a scheme may have an impressive religious exterior, our private desires for wanting the change may be far from honourable.

Some people may want to bring change into a church in order to improve their own status. At least one young man in the history of church life has proposed starting a new group or adopting a new evangelistic programme, partially in the hope that the middle-aged and older leadership will at least notice he exists, and that members of the larger church will perhaps get to know his name. Suggesting change may also be a way for a woman to receive some recognition in a male-dominated church.

Other people may wish to introduce change because they have something to prove, not just to the church, but to their own families and to themselves. They may want to be seen to be displaying an aggressively active Christian life in order to cover up a superficial and empty spirituality within. 'If I do all this, and suggest all this, it proves that I must be fine as a Christian.'

There are others who, because of an extremely low self-image, cannot bathe in God's unconditional love. This last group are frantically hoping to achieve some worth by trying to earn God's approval.

Our motives, sadly, are never pure. But we should never try to introduce change until we can honestly say before God that, as far as we can judge, we want to change things because of a genuine desire to extend his kingdom. We need to be able to say that by seeking to bring about this change, we are working to enable God's will to be better done on earth as it is in heaven (Matthew 6:10).

Be humble

We have already argued the need for humility when holding opinions because our understanding of spiritual truth is not yet perfect. We have to recognize that the changes we want to introduce may be misguided and that it is the job of the church to assess them. If the church rejects our ideas, it may be because we are wrong and they are right. Churches sometimes need the wisdom, grace and strength to say 'No' or 'No, not yet.'

There is another reason for suggesting change with humility. People are much less likely to feel immediately threatened by what we are saying if we approach them humbly, rather than with an arrogance which says, 'I'm right and you're wrong.' With humility it is difficult to rub people up the wrong way; without it you will almost certainly kill any chances of an easy acceptance of your ideas.

Be prayerful

When wanting to change a situation, we can become pre-occupied with the apparent failings of certain people. They start to 'get under our skin'. Worship and fellowship with them are strained to say the least. What usually happens is that we want to fight *them*, seeing *them* as the cause of all our problems.

While we do not want to diminish the role of individual responsibility for sin in any way, all of us should recognize that it is the spiritual forces for evil in the heavenly realms that are tempting them and us to sin. We should be fighting a spiritual battle with prayer (Ephesians 6:12), not a physical one with cold shoulders.

That argument about carpets and chairs was essentially a spiritual one. You wanted comfortable chairs to replace the hard, narrow pews. And you wanted the building carpeted. It wasn't just for your comfort. You were concerned about the image that the church gave to outsiders. Some of your non-Christian friends had come to a service once and had complained about the cold and the pews. Of course, Satan used some people in the church to resist you. He doesn't want the church to be a welcoming place where people might come, be converted, stay, and grow in grace. The more excuses he can give them for not coming the better!

Pray change through. It won't always make it easier, or even necessarily take away all the resistance, but it will help you to rely on God and to keep 'clean hands' throughout. It is the only way to achieve lasting success.

Assess the importance of the issue

One of the smoke alarms in our house seems to go off every time the oven is on. The food is usually great; it's just that the alarm is too sensitive. Some of us, similarly, seem to be able to sprinkle anger with plenty of noise around the church at the slightest provocation. We need to adjust our sensitivity threshold, or we'll start to look ridiculous.

One man was angry, negative, and over-zealous in his criticism at almost every church business meeting that had taken place since soon after he came to the church over five years ago. He was tolerated, but rarely taken seriously. Another lady had spent twenty years with the church, and during that time she had only once been heard to be critical of the church leadership. When she was, everybody, including the leaders, listened with great care to what she said.

Learn to assess
- whether something is likely to really lead the church into doctrinal error and bring dishonour to God,
- or whether something is just different from what you have been used to, but is nevertheless perfectly legitimate for Christians to do.

If, like General Custer, you want to take a last stand against the 'enemy', choose something important, and don't end up fighting your own Christian family. If you're going to get angry, get angry over something which will clearly make God angry. The position in which the arms are held during worship doesn't really merit the amount of heat it can generate between brothers and sisters in Christ.

Seek the opinion of others

'Make plans by seeking advice' (Proverbs 20:18a).

One of the best ways of assessing the wisdom of an idea is to present it to others who are objective enough to be able to evaluate it, and loving enough to give you an honest answer. It's easy to be a great thinker in a small pond. Try swimming in a bigger river and see what the pikes make of your ideas.

We're not for a moment suggesting that you immediately run round everybody in the church and try out your ideas on them. All that may achieve is putting some of them off right from the start. It may be wise to consult a select few people in the church at a later stage. What we are suggesting here is that you consult a few wise and discreet Christian friends who are outside your immediate situation, preferably from another church, and ideally from another town.

Because you're in the situation, you're sometimes blind to points that others can see clearly. That's why new people coming into a church often want to shake things up. They can see things which the existing congregation just doesn't notice or regard as important.

It may be that the advice you receive will help you modify your original ideas. Praise God for people who can say, 'Yes, I think it's a great idea. Your church seems to need to do something in that area. From my limited knowledge of your congregation, though, I don't think what you're suggesting would work as it stands. It's too ... Why not try ...' If your advisers support your ideas, it will help give you peace and determination in the face of inevitable opposition. If your advisers tell you to drop the idea, listen to their advice but go on thinking and praying.

Choose your words with care

However strongly you may feel about something, learn to avoid unnecessary conflict through the wise choice of words. Our language can cause as much damage as a sword (Psalm 57:4; Proverbs 12:18). We have a tendency to put the responsibility for problems on to other people. Our language often reflects that spirit of blame. That approach provokes people to become defensive and to counter-attack. Before we realize what has happened, much hurt has been caused, and we have a row on our hands. Another way of tackling the problem would be to focus on our own response to the situation, regardless of what others are doing.

Suppose someone suggests closing the Sunday School and replacing it with a mid-week youth activity. If you disagree with this, you may use the emotive words, 'You are wrong', which is likely to cause some resentment. You are blaming somebody else for the sense of unease that is being experienced, and you are implying, 'I am right.' A much less threatening response would be to say: 'I have a problem with that suggestion because ...' You are clearly owning the difficulty and not trying to blame the other person. You are also talking honestly about your feelings, which will tend to promote understanding. Such a response is less likely to lead to conflict.

Be persuasive

'Don't go charging into battle without a plan' (Proverbs 20:18b, GNB).

The initial hostility to some suggestions for change may appear to be completely irrational, and people may change their minds for emotional reasons. Lasting change, by contrast, is likely to engage people's understanding. Any claim that God has told someone that the church needs to do something should be evaluated by the leadership, but if most congregations are to be convinced, good reasons will need to be given. Do what Nehemiah did before rebuilding the walls of Jerusalem. Survey the situation. Think through the following areas:

- What is the biblical support for the idea? Is there support from a range of passages, or does the idea come from a rather strained interpretation of one passage?
- Is there a need now, in this church, for what is being suggested?
- What are the personnel implications? Are there enough people in the church? Would people need to be trained? Would it mean already overworked people becoming even more overworked? Both Joseph and Nehemiah had to face similar questions in their respective work of feeding a nation and of rebuilding a city.
- What are the short-term and long-term financial implications for the church? Would it be wiser to spend the church's money in other ways? The writer of Proverbs commends financial planning because wealth is an impermanent resource that has to be used wisely (Proverbs 27:23–27).
- What are other churches doing about this? Can you find examples of similar practices so that you can learn from the success or mistakes of others?

If you want to build a tower, and if you want others to help you, sit down and count the cost. Saying 'The Lord told me to build' isn't usually enough! Noah had his own family to convince about the ark, but he didn't have to persuade your PCC or diaconate!

Be understanding

Accept that people will object to your proposals, and that some will have genuine fears. Try to anticipate those objections. Put yourself in the shoes of your likely critics. What might you be afraid of if you were them? Whenever there's anger, look for the pain.

If you are given a chance to argue your case don't just include the kind of material we have suggested above. Make a point of attempting to answer your critics. It shows them that you take seriously what they are thinking, and you may provide them with a perspective that they hadn't seen before. For instance:

> *I know many of you might be unhappy about changing the time of the midweek prayer meeting from 7:30 to 7:45. It's always been at 7:30, and some of you have real fears that if it went on past 9:30 it would mean some people getting home very late. But that extra fifteen minutes would make it so much easier for those of us who are struggling to get children to bed, and it wouldn't necessarily mean that we would have to go on past 9:30. If we started promptly each week, and cut out one of the choruses, I'm sure we could still finish before 9:30. We often finish praying well before 9:15 as it is at the moment.*

Be specific

Don't pepper meetings with shotgun blasts. Get a rifle and

94

show some real skill in aiming. The more specific you are with your suggestions, the more likely they are to be listened to seriously.

Too vague and negative:
> *The worship is awful!*

Better:
> *Could we try learning some new songs from XYZ Songbook at our housegroups, and have one in every service?*

Too vague and negative:
> *This church is doing nothing about evangelism.*

Better:
> *Let's invite the playgroups in the area, and the contacts we already have through the youth group, to a family fun barbeque on a Saturday in June. We could produce the invitations ourselves on the wordprocessor. And perhaps either Christine or Peter could speak, or we could invite that evangelist . . .*

Too vague and negative:
> *The housegroups are terrible!*

Better:
> *Perhaps we could ask the leadership team to have a look at this new group material. It really does seem to have some interesting ideas for getting people talking and praying together.*

Be persistent

Our strategy needs to be soft, strong, and very long! Many of us are too impatient. We want instantaneous results. If only everybody could immediately see it our way! Although we may experience frustration and delays, God is able to use that time in at least two ways.

First, it may be that what we want to do is wrong. The resistance we experience should cause us to think and pray carefully about what we are doing. God may use people in the church to show us that what we wanted was misconceived on this occasion.

Secondly, God can use even sinful resistance for his glory. Such opposition can cause us to depend more closely on him, and he can mature our characters as we learn patience in suffering.

Think about the frustrations Jesus must have experienced with the disciples. Their limited understanding about his kingdom seemed so slow to develop, and we would have been no different. They were in a rut. Time and time again he tried to teach them about how to change things through faith, about how he must suffer and rise again, and about how his reign would not be in an earthly territory. Be encouraged by his example (Mark 8). Despite the frustrations, Jesus brought glory to his Father by completing the work he had been given (John 17:4).

And think about the alternative – namely, giving up. If we give up it will take even longer for change to come, and that is not only bad for the church, but dishonouring to God if we are acting as his instrument. It took one pastor nearly ten years to get his church to accept that women should be allowed to pray in public meetings. Now many people in the church are so glad that he didn't give up.

Be submissive

One of the best ways of ensuring that change is extremely painful, or that it fails completely, is to try to bring it about by bypassing the leadership of the church. If the leadership says 'No', we shouldn't try to go over their heads and appeal directly to the 'voters'. The body should be in submission to its leaders and not in a state of uncoordinated anarchy.

We may feel that the leadership has made a mistake in its judgment. Unless such judgments are leading us into sin, however, we are commanded to submit to them (Hebrews 13:17). We cannot be held responsible for our leaders' actions and thinking (God will judge them for that). But we do have a clear responsibility for our own actions and thinking, and should seek to obey Christ in obeying them.

Happy Fields Independent Evangelical Church had always held a weekly open-air evangelistic meeting in the park during summer. There were often a few courting couples, people with dogs, and a few families who walked quickly by as the Word was proclaimed by suited men with black Bibles. The pastor thought modern Christian music trite, and strongly opposed women speakers. Reg, who was given the task of organizing the meetings, was frustrated. He could see that something needed to be done, but wasn't sure what, and, knowing the pastor's views, felt unable to change anything.

And then Clive and Marion came to the church. Nobody was quite sure why they stayed! They seemed so lively and full of ideas. Both of them had preached in their last church, and the general feeling was that Marion was more gifted than Clive. They were also extremely good singers.

'I know,' thought Reg. 'I'll use Marion in the next open-air. She can sing and then give her testimony.' He mentioned to the pastor what he was thinking and received a short, sharp rebuttal, which in non-Christian circles would have been regarded as rude. In a fit of pique, which Reg was to regret for years, he went ahead with Marion anyway. She really was good and communicated her message powerfully.

By the next day the pastor had relieved Reg of his responsibility for the open-airs, and at least four discernible groups within the church had emerged. It would be over a year before the body began to feel whole again.

There were those who supported the pastor's judgment and were scandalized that a woman should be preaching at one of their open-airs. There were those who didn't really have any strong views either way about women preachers, but who were scandalized by the way Reg had gone against the pastor, and were supporting the pastor. There were those who were scandalized that the pastor should object to Marion speaking, and who, in the light of this incident, were dragging out all their other disagreements with him. And again, there were those who didn't have any strong view either way about the issue itself, but were horrified by the way Reg had been treated.

Seven years later Clive and Marion were put in charge of the open-air outreach and they introduced changes in the venue, the timing, the music, the speakers. No, the pastor hadn't left the church, but Clive and Marion had spent eight years praying regularly for him. They also often invited him and his wife round for supper so that they could chat and pray together. Each 'side' had developed respect and trust for the other.

Change is a threatening but necessary experience. Donald Bridge has observed that people facing it 'will either curl up like a hedgehog, prickles outward, or fight back with all the ferocity of instinct opposed to logic'.[1] Let's embrace and take part in God's continuing work of changing his church, despite the prickles and the bruises.

CHAPTER 9

A CREEPING DESERT

It is a Thursday evening in July. The time for the mid-week meeting is drawing near, but the people who normally go are strangely reluctant to leave their televisions (yes, even in July, and Wimbledon is over) or their gardens. The unspoken thought is, 'I feel negative enough about the church as it is, without going to another meeting and reminding myself. I'll only come home feeling worse.'

Like the gardens, the prayer meetings have become dry and dusty. Sundays are worse, and the conversation at the last church picnic was so carefully superficial it was painful. Not that there has been a major row (that was last year!) or anything much to put your finger on. But the people feel they are in a desert.

Two miles away another meeting has already begun. About a dozen people are sitting on a strange variety of armchairs, kitchen stools and floor cushions, looking expectantly at their home group leader. He is going to introduce the next study in the series they are doing on the Holy Spirit. People have already benefited so much from their discussions and shared discoveries, as they have looked afresh at what the Bible says, that there is a genuine readiness to learn which excites them all – all except Bob. Of course, he does his best to join in as much as he can, but in reality, that is very little.

Bob is sitting in 'darkness'. It seems to him that no amount of light or love can penetrate. And all the while, the same inescapable messages of loss, overwhelming disappointment and bewilderment spin round his tired and heavy head. Bob is in his own personal desert.

What is a desert?

Deserts are places 'without . . .', whether we are describing physical or spiritual realities. Most obviously, a physical desert is a place without water, where survival is a struggle. Spiritual deserts are not described so easily, but a common factor might be that the joy of knowing God has gone. Certainly, survival is difficult and painful. Theologically we may know that God keeps his promises, and we cannot fall away into eternal damnation, but our inner thoughts and feelings scream the opposite. It is the experience of living in a desert that we discuss in this chapter, together with the questions 'How and why did I get here?' and 'Do I adapt or move out?' In the next chapter we consider practical strategies for surviving in a desert. For now, though, we concentrate on getting our bearings.

Desert feelings

There are several levels of desert experience, one of which is typified by David in Psalm 63.

> O God, you are my God,
> earnestly I seek you;

> my soul longs for you,
>> my body longs for you,
> in a dry and weary land
>> where there is no water.
>>> *(verse 1)*

This is the level at which most of the people in the church described at the start of the chapter are living. They long to feel God's presence as they used to. They feel that same spiritual dryness and long to do something about it. They remember God's love clearly, and have no doubt that he still loves them, will rescue them eventually, and will act justly. Their desert is real, but it has not yet begun to eat into their souls with conviction-destroying persistence.

Another psalmist writes out of a deeper despair in Psalm 88:

> For my soul is full of trouble
>> and my life draws near the grave.
> I am counted among those who go down to the pit;
>> I am like a man without strength.
> I am set apart with the dead,
>> like the slain who lie in the grave,
> whom you remember no more,
>> who are cut off from your care.
>>> *(verses 3–5)*

This man has lived with dread and despair so long that his awareness of God's anger is more real than his memories of God's grace. This is more than dryness; this is isolation, panic, bewilderment, and hopelessness. He feels so helpless, he may as well be dead.

Remember the law of 'reverse encouragement' from chapter 3? Here it is in operation, by God's design. These psalms (and others around the same theme) were put in the Bible to help us when we are 'going through it'. If we can just bring ourselves to open the Bible, we can find our very worst thoughts already there, probably expressed more forcefully than we would dare to. They don't write Christian songs like that any more!

How did I get into the desert – and why?

On the radio programme *Desert Island Discs*, the questions are mostly fun.

'What is the one record you would take, if you couldn't take all eight?'

'One luxury – what would it be?'

'Which book would you like to have on the island, assuming that the Bible and the Complete Works of Shakespeare are already there?'

Even if we take 'desert' to mean 'deserted', the island sounds more like the sort of haven people dream about, than a place to eke out a precarious existence. An island which is spiritually desert (in both senses) is surrounded by soul-searching and even soul-destroying questions that are no fun at all.

'How did this happen?'

'Where *were* you, God?'

'Are you punishing me/us for something?'

'Where do I/we go from here?'

'What if I don't want to go on with you, what then?'

Coping with church life during a time of dryness is tough, whether it is the whole body that is parched or whether it is just yourself. In the desert, prayers seem to disappear without trace. We are still left asking 'Why?'

There are so many possible reasons for a desert that we hesitate to give any at all here. Nevertheless, we offer few suggestions, not in the hope of mirroring your own case exactly, but in the hope that you might recognize some danger signals in your life or the lives of your Christian sisters and brothers.

Sinner and sinned against

Christians are not exempt from the effects of sin, either their own or someone else's. It can be devastating. (It *is* devastating; that's why we need Jesus in the first place.) If you are the victim, everything in you cries out 'Unfair!' and you grow tired and discouraged, even bitter and cynical, looking for justice to arrive. Then you realize that it won't, in the form you want; God doesn't work in that way.

If you are the one who has created the wasteland, by giving in to that sin you hoped to keep under control, you are desperate for damage limitation at any cost. Pretending it wasn't you, moving 200 miles away, or ceasing to exist are just some of the options you consider. Then you realize that to take any one of these courses would only spread the desert area, not contain it.

Lack of forgiveness is a much covered-up sin that wreaks havoc among Christians. A church may have the unseen worm of unacknowledged, unforgiven sin eating away at it, affecting the innocent as well as the guilty, and creating spiritual barrenness. Likewise a friendship, a marriage or a family may grind along for years in a desert or on its margins, without anyone having the courage to bring Jesus' life, death and resurrection into the relationship(s).

Changed circumstances

Sometimes there is no sin involved (except in the sense that we live in a fallen, imperfect world). People may find themselves in a wilderness after someone close to them has died – a parent, perhaps, or a real friend or an unborn baby. An accident may lead to permanent disability. Failure to reach a required standard in exams or tests of competence may result in the loss of career hopes. Many things can create a personal desert.

In a church, all sorts of events may combine to leave the people gasping and struggling. Someone gets a promotion and a key family in the church moves away; another person gets married and also moves away; three couples all have babies; a very elderly and holy person dies. In a small church just one of these can be enough to disrupt its life seriously.

Trying too hard?

In between the two extreme of a desert caused by blatant sin and one caused by changed circumstances there is a range of factors which, even if they do not create a desert on their own, certainly help the climate to move in that direction. Anger, depression, over-busyness, mixed-up priorities and guilt all come under this heading.

Debbie and Peter are simply tired out. New to parenthood, the novelty of multiple broken nights wore off long ago. Peter is desperate to prove to everyone what a good father he is, while Debbie is equally desperately trying to keep up with her Sunday School preparation and teaching. Everyone praises their efforts and 'encourages' them, unwittingly digging the pit a bit deeper. Debbie and Peter are starting to feel the desert encroaching, and they are afraid.

Sue is in her second year at university. She plays squash once a week with her non-Christian friend; she attends two Christian Union meetings a week, often leading a Bible study, and has recently joined a 'witnessing team' in the church she attends. Sue is also conscientious about her studies. Somehow, she has become committed to too many things and cannot see the honourable way out of any of them, especially as she 'felt led' to take on each one. Consequently, Sue is secretly beginning to resent God and the demands he makes on her. She feels strangely depressed, and does not understand why God seems further away these days.

Ron can cope with all the Christian responsibilities that are being put on to him. His desert is growing because his motivation for doing them has changed. He is on automatic pilot and has lost his close dependence on God for strength.

These people have to find the courage to re-examine *and change* their priorities soon. Anyone who has tried this will know how difficult it is, but carrying on as if everything is 'just fine' is no substitute.

People may find their existence as Christians threatened by dryness, or worse, for all sorts of reasons. And in some cases, the answer to the question 'Why, Lord, and for how long?' remains unanswered. Then you need to ask some different questions, such as, 'What is it about me that cannot cope with this?' (particularly valuable in a 'church desert'), and 'What can I learn while I am here?'

Adapt to the desert or move out?

If living in a desert is going to be such a valuable experience, mustn't it be right to stay there and make the best of it?

Certainly, when we're in a situation where there is a lack of spiritual life, we may not want to stay put. We may be tempted to think, 'It's dry, it's painful, it cannot be what God wants for me. I'm off!' In chapters 11 and 12, we explore the issue involved in leaving your church.

In the case of a personal desert, it must be said that a move away of some sort is sometimes advisable – a different job, a new neighbourhood, a relationship terminated. But a physical move doesn't necessarily take you out of the personal desert. You may take your desert with you.

If, for instance, your love-relationship with the Lord has dwindled away to nothing, you will have to find out how

105

to gain the will and the confidence to restore it, wherever you go. You may not want to do anything about it at all, of course. Admit it, there are times when you can't help thinking that life would be a lot easier and more pleasant if you were not a Christian. But because God is faithful, even in the face of our most blatant unfaithfulness, he will persevere with you until you *do* want to do something about it. He will love you until you respond.

Another argument that we may use to justify leaving a spiritually barren situation is this. We tell ourselves: 'I might get used to the desert. I might accept marginal existence as the norm. I might even get to like it.'

This is a real danger. It sounds paradoxical, but it is possible to make yourself almost comfortable in a spiritual wilderness. Perhaps this is because it provides the perfect excuse for a low level of commitment to the Lord. No-one can expect too much of you in *those* circumstances. You may reason that, in the desert, plants do not routinely flourish and bear fruit, they just hang on until the next shower.

After successfully rationalizing your desert situation, and discovering that you can survive, you might just begin to feel pleased with yourself, and look down (secretly) on those who crack under the strain. Pride is insidious. It sneaks its way into the most unlikely situations. Now you are in danger of becoming a cactus – a very successful desert plant, but hardly cuddly. Surely, the same principles of humility, love, encouragement and serving others apply in a desert as elsewhere? Rather than immediately leaving the situation, or allowing it to mould your character, we would suggest that you aim, humbly, to shape the desert.

Although it's natural to want to come out of periods of personal dryness, there are at least three positive reasons for staying put in barren circumstances.

The first is that survival *is* possible. When all ordinary comforts are stripped away, then the reality (or otherwise) of your Christian life is laid bare. This can be incredibly painful.

Justin had enjoyed several useful and mostly happy years in his church. He was committed to the fellowship and a respected member of it. Then a combination of events caused his world to fall to pieces. In his isolation, Justin found there was nothing but his relationship with God to sustain him: no fellowship, no teaching that made any sense, nothing to give, no way of serving. Justin was shocked to discover how minimal his love for God was, now that everything else had gone. In fact, he was questioning whether a God of love really existed at all (even though he knew all the right answers). Justin loathed his desert and felt he was entitled to reject the God who had put him there.

But Justin hung on grimly, telling God just what he thought. As the months went by, he found that he was surviving the harsh desert conditions. He had a growing hunger and thirst for reality with the Lord, even while he still doubted it was possible for him personally.

A few years later, Justin was able, just about, to explain how he could be grateful for those hard times, because he had learned the basics of being a Christian on a deeper level. 'The grace of God' would never be just words for him again.

The first argument for adapting to a desert, then, is that you learn, or relearn, survival as a Christian. The second follows on from that: you can help others to survive and also receive help from them. This is particularly true when the whole church is going through a dry time. There will be people who, like you, are wondering how to remain a Christian *and* cope with the church. It is a time to be honest with God and with yourself. Out of this honesty, new understanding, humility, compassion, and forgiveness can grow.

Even if you are going through the desert alone, you will still be able to help others at some stage. Sometimes, being in a wilderness brings a renewed awareness of what it is like to be totally without God in the world, which bears fruit later in your friendships with non-Christians. Or when someone who is now going through the kind of desert you were in a few years ago turns to you, you are far less likely to rush in with easy answers and cliché solutions.

The third argument for staying, rather than attempting to flee, is this: you learn there what God wants you to learn. This probably seems obvious to you, if you are looking at the whole topic objectively. If, however, you have recently left a green and pleasant land and now find yourself in a howling wilderness, it is not at all obvious. You are bound to feel at best uncertain, and at worst panic-stricken. Whether the dryness is all within you or primarily in your church, it seems highly unlikely that any spiritual growth will take place. But by God's grace, you will find your character being developed, albeit slowly, in new and unsuspected areas.

Janice had always been ambitious and confident. She was delighted when she gained a promotion, even though it meant moving away. Then, just before she left, it came to light that a close friend in her fellowship group had repeatedly deceived and tricked her. A few days later, Janice was in a new house with a new job and a new, unwelcome emptiness where love and trust used to be.

To fill up the void in her life, she volunteered to help a well-known, but secular, charitable organization which had a strong base in the area. Before long, Janice found herself facing all sorts of new and unexpected challenges. She had to develop new skills, and she also had to face some hard questions (mostly put to Janice by Janice) about her faith. Slowly, although most of the inner desert remained, Janice began to experience a strange joy as she discovered that she could stop neither believing in God, nor loving him. That was just the beginning. The desert conditions were forcing her to move in a different direction. In other words, Janice

108

was seeing the things God wanted her to see, growing and learning as she went along.

If you are in a desert, take comfort from the fact that there are many people in the Bible who will be able to identify with your circumstances. Job, for example, suffered a long period of spiritual turmoil without ever really understanding why, and many psalms reflect David's own anguish. The point is that deserts aren't necessarily destructive to Christians. God can use them for his own purposes of strengthening and maturing. In the next chapter we suggest some practical strategies for survival in a desert.

10

SURVIVAL IN A DESERT

We've seen how it feels to be in a spiritual desert, some possible reasons for being there, and some benefits that can come out of what seems to be a wholly negative experience. But what can you do, practically, in your own rather dreadful circumstances? Here are some strategies that have worked for us.

Oases, underground tubers and condensation

This is the point at which we cannot resist extending the desert analogy a little further. People who live in deserts have to look for water in strange places. They do not walk around listlessly, complaining that there are no rivers. Instead, they work to find what they need. They travel long distances to find oases. They dig for tubers with moisture hoarded inside. They dig in old, dry river beds until a muddy puddle appears. They learn to use every drop of water, wherever they find it. Christians who are going through difficult times need to learn where to find 'spiritual water' too, when the usual sources have dried up.

The oasis strategy

A few years ago we, as a family, felt dry, discouraged and tired of tired Christianity. In desperation, we overcame our prejudices and booked a 'holiday' at a large Christian teaching and celebration event. Quite contrary to our expectations, those few days in a freezing east-coast resort at Easter proved to be an oasis. It turned out that God was alive and well after all. More than that, he still had a place for us in his kingdom and work for us to do.

Visiting an oasis is immensely refreshing. It need not be quite so drastic as a whole week of Christian holiday/conference either. A Sunday seeing friends and going to church with them, a Christian 'marriage weekend' (if you are married), a trip 'home' when that is still somewhere other than the place you live – these are all examples of visits to oases. You may be able to think of another one, more fitted to your circumstances.

Unfortunately, there are drawbacks to the oasis strategy. You have to travel – you cannot live there. The experience of the oasis is heightened, because it is a special occasion and everyone is likely to be making an extra effort. Afterwards, your everyday existence may seem even worse, by contrast. This is not to say that you should avoid opportunities to refresh your spirit in this way; God likes you to be happy and enjoy yourself! But you need to have other ways of surviving, right where you are.

The digging strategy

When the desert takes over where you used to find 'rivers of living water' (or at least a steady trickle) running through your own devotions, your service for the Lord, and your fellowship in your church, you now need to look for drops – and make the most of them.

One of our friends developed what we called the 'one thought' strategy. He was so good at this that we used to joke that he would find a drop of moisture in a stone (code-word for impenetrable sermon)!

If you are struggling through a season of dry sermons you could try practising the art of digging for that one drop (idea) that interests you, or strikes some chord of sympathy in you; something that you can relate to personally. Spend time with that one thought, asking why it caught your attention and meditating on what God might have to say about it. This is a much more positive thing to do than focusing on all that you found dull!

One way to make the most of 'drops' is to discover how to be thankful for them. That is really tough to do too. You most likely want to complain, not say, 'Praise the Lord!' Not that we are advising a mindless utterance, or some attempt to pretend to God that everything in the garden is lovely. He can see it is a desert just as well as you. What we are saying is 'Practise being positive' as well as honest. We shall say more about this at the end of the chapter.

Another way to maximize the benefit of the small amount of 'spiritual water' you have found is to recycle it: share it generously and humbly with someone else. Unlike ordinary water, this doubles the amount you have, rather than halving it!

You need not try to be entirely self-sufficient when digging for water either. Try talking – but mostly listening – to the older people in the church family. Not only will you encourage them, you will also come to have a broader perspective. It often happens that they have been through the same thing as you three of four times. Even if they have not, it is fascinating to hear about their experiences. Best of all you might make a new friend.

It is very hard to enjoy your private times with God when your spirit is parched. Just when you most need it, prayer feels impossible and the Bible seems (dare we say it?) boring. Sometimes you can be revived by making quite a simple change in your quiet-time routine:

- a different time of day;
- a different place, such as in the garden;
- an unfamiliar version of the Bible;
- different Bible reading notes;
- no Bible reading notes at all;
- a structured programme of study involving written responses, such as that offered by a correspondence course;[1]
- using a concordance to study a topic or theme, rather than reading through a chapter or a book;
- sharing your prayer and reading time with a Christian friend or member of your family.

These are just a few of the possibilities.

But what if the problem is that no time of day is a good time? Try promising yourself and the Lord just two minutes every day for a week. It sounds shockingly minimal to anyone brought up to believe that an hour before breakfast is the only thing acceptable to God or man. But it is a whole two minutes better than no time at all, and may grow to something longer.

Some of us, living in a desert for a long time, lose touch with our own souls. We are so busy, or tired, or preoccupied, or in pain, that we can hardly think straight, let alone pray. Then we need to find a means of gaining insight into our hearts. Here are some strategies we've found helpful.

- Read Christian books, especially biographies.[2]
- Learn some new Christian music. Listen to praise tapes when travelling (but keep your hands on the wheel!)
- Use books of 'ready-made' prayers. (It's not cheating and it can help tremendously, especially if your own

113

prayers bounce back off the ceiling.) If you're not part of a denomination that has a liturgy, give a friend a shock by asking to borrow a copy of a prayer book.

■ Keep an informal journal, perhaps in the form of letters to God. Do try to be honest and don't try to be 'super-spiritual'. Nevertheless, be prepared to find the Lord using your journal to help you understand yourself and his dealings with you.

If you are able to fast, it can be one way of showing God that you are serious about meeting with him. When you are deeply concerned about the aridity in your church, for instance, and you want to do something to help, consider the combination of prayer and fasting. You will make a positive contribution to the situation and will also give the Lord the opportunity to do the same – through you!

The melting ice strategy

In the novel *Flight of the Phoenix*,[3] an aircraft crashes in a desert. The survivors discover that if a parachute is laid out on the ground at night, condensation gathers on the underside. It then freezes in the low temperatures – providing a meagre source of drinking water the next day. (There is probably no direct spiritual equivalent, although we did once hear someone pray, 'Thank you for the glorious condensation of our Lord Jesus Christ'!)

The idea of the melting ice strategy is to look for truth, joy and encouragement in unusual places. Sometimes we make the mistake of thinking or acting as if Christians had a monopoly on these things, whereas they are to be found all over the place, once you start looking. We are not talking about doctrinal truth here, but rather the God-given insights that many people have, although they do not recognize the giver. As something helpful and useful to do in the desert, the exercise works too. Here is one person's testimony:

Since I began looking for truth and goodness in 'the world', I have been amazed and humbled to see generosity, willingness to forgive, sheer kindness and many other qualities shown by friends and neighbours. At one time, I would only have felt uneasy 'because they are not Christians', but now I tell the Lord how glad I am to see these evidences of his goodness and gracious love.

Another way open to some people is to get involved in the local community, for example on a village hall or community centre committee, in a school or playgroup, in local government, through a local Voluntary Service Bureau, in a sports club or at the YMCA. There are opportunities here to be salt and light, simply by living out Christian principles and values in public, instead of behind church doors. Who knows, someone may even ask you about your faith, one day.

Take a new walk

As we said earlier, deserts are places 'without . . .', described in negative terms. Your thoughts, as they revolve around your difficulties, become increasingly negative. To get away from the desert metaphor, let's picture your thought life in a different way.

You are walking round and round a rubbish dump. It is smelly, dirty, even dangerous, and a lot of it sticks to you. This is the inner environment you are creating for yourself when you habitually (and it can even be subconsciously) think negatively about your problems.

What you need to do, when you realize your thoughts are taking you this way, is to map out a different route. The new walk is towards something attractive, beautiful and good to see. It may be a very short walk at first, because you are uncertain and unused to taking the positive path, but practice will enhance your courage and whet your appetite for more.

This plan for your thought life is not something sub-Christian, but thoroughly biblical.

> Finally, brothers, whatever is true, whatever is noble, whatever is right, whatever is pure, whatever is lovely, whatever is admirable – if anything is excellent or praiseworthy – think about such things.
>
> *(Philippians 4:8)*

Because of the sheer force of habit, you will need to do three things to prevent your thoughts taking their usual route into unhealthy negativity.

1. Spend some time planning your new route carefully, so that it is all ready for when you need it.
2. Learn to recognize what sets you off on the rubbish-dump walk.
3. Put up some big signs in your mind saying 'DIVERSION' or 'NATURE TRAIL' or 'WALK THIS WAY PLEASE', to remind yourself to take the new route. (You may be surprised at how many times a day you need them.)

Robyn was so overwhelmed by problems with her children's behaviour, both in church and outside, that it affected most of her day, and a sizeable portion of the night. She could hardly even pray, because it just turned into one long moan and got no further. Then she heard of the 'new walk' and began something like this:

'Why does Bobby have to be so difficult? Bobby is [new walk] ... healthy ... active(!) ... known by the Lord ... loves the dog ... thank you for Bobby.'

116

It didn't seem much of a start, but it proved to be a turning point.

Meryl, a hard-worked and under-appreciated church treasurer, tried a similar strategy:

> *'Why does no-one realize that I'm stretched to the limit as it is, without bringing in all these changes? I'm fed up with this church! The church is [new walk] . . . well, there is Mrs C., she is a dear . . . she gives so sacrificially too . . . Thank you for the way Mr C. and others give of themselves . . . not just money . . . Thank you for the way the church is growing . . .'*

These are not meant to be model 'new walks', but they are meant to give some idea of how to start. A 'new walk' for our thoughts begins with something *true*. That is very important, as much of our rubbishy 'old walk' is around half-truths and exaggerations (lies, in other words). The new route goes on to something else good. It may or may not focus on God's input, but it probably will, with practice. It may eventually end up somewhere very near to thanking God and even praising him.

Note how different this is from the counterfeit 'positive thinking' of secular humanism. It is also different from the empty 'Never mind, there is always someone worse off than you', or the maddening 'Cheer up, it may never happen!' proffered as comfort by some. It is different because it focuses on truth and directs us to God's presence in the problems. Taking charge of your thought life is the key to the success of all the other survival methods we have discussed.

Seeing the desert grow greener

Justin, mentioned in the previous chapter, found himself thinking of God as the 'Big Baddy' who pulled out the plug and left him high and dry. This is not uncommon. We want to make God responsible for what has happened to us. And of course, in way, he is! Incredible as it may seem, God allows us, and the people around us, to make the most stupid mistakes, to struggle on blindly, to get trapped by sin, and so on. Whatever we know about our own responsibility for our situation, we can still say, 'Well, God let it happen.'

At this point you will not be surprised to find the usual text, Romans 8:28, 'trundled out' to explain what is going on. But before you groan, look carefully at the preceding verses.

> In the same way, the Spirit helps us in our weakness. We do not know what we ought to pray for, but the Spirit himself intercedes for us with groans that words cannot express. And he who searches our hearts knows the mind of the Spirit, because the Spirit intercedes for the saints in accordance with God's will.
>
> And we know that in all things God works for the good of those who love him, who have been called according to his purpose.
>
> *(Romans 8:26–28)*

These verses show us a *real* glimpse behind the scenes. Far from revealing God as a hard-hearted, unfeeling and distant manipulator of our pain and confusion, they show how the Holy Spirit of God himself is there, feeling our agony and communicating our deepest needs to the Father.

It is true that God 'let it happen', but it is equally true that he is with you, even within you, while it happens and for as long as it lasts. If you'll forgive the pun, God does not desert you in the desert. A friend of ours[4] is fond of saying, 'God is more interested in your character than your comfort.' In order to catch and hold our attention, the Lord of our lives may have to let us get really uncomfortable; only then will he work on that aspect of our character that has caught *his* attention.

It is important to fully grasp that, however much we plan *our* strategies for survival through spiritual Saharas, it is the fact that '*God* works . . .' (Romans 8:28) that ensures that we come through at all. The desert will become greener, and even become swallowed up, but it will always be God's power (within us and without us!) that makes it happen. As Paul wrote to a church threatened by in-fighting, 'I planted the seed, Apollos watered it, but God made it grow' (1 Corinthians 3:6). Paul was talking about the seed of the gospel which took root in their hearts. He called their church 'God's field' (1 Corinthians 3:9), and that is what your church is too, God's own piece of land, specially marked out for his cultivation.

Will you cope with the desert? Will you cling on to life and hope by the tips of your fingernails? Realize that God is more than equal to the task of helping you to cope and to come through.

Earlier, we quoted from Psalm 63, a 'desert song'. Here is a profound truth expressed later in the psalm:

> My soul clings to you;
> your right hand upholds me.
> *(verse 8)*

We may feel our grip slipping; we may even feel we have let go. Yet God can and will hold us, and continue to hold us, because he is everlastingly loving and faithful.

CHAPTER 11

THINKING OF LEAVING A CHURCH?

The Sunday School outing scandal

There is at least one occasion when it is clearly right to leave a church. If your minister goes on the Sunday School outing to the beach and runs around wearing nothing but trunks or swimsuit, you should leave your church immediately. How can you respect the preaching and pastoral leadership of such a person?

Yes, you're right. We *are* joking! (Even so, we won't be too surprised to receive at least one letter saying that this incident actually happened.)

Some people leave churches for strange reasons. The more extraordinary the reason given for leaving, the more probable it is that the people concerned should stay in their present church.

Getting, going, giving

One of the dangers that we might fall into is that of adopting a consumerist attitude to churches. We see them as 'places to get certain things', rather than as 'families to belong to', or 'places to be servants and become more like Christ'.

To some extent it is right that we should evaluate the quality of what they give us. As has been argued in chapters 1, 2 and 3, we want churches to be places that will actually help us in our Christian growth. Sometimes, however, we become overcritical and fastidious in our evaluation. We become so concerned with the tiny details of what we are getting or not getting, that we lose sight of bigger things, such as loyalty, commitment, and service. We become fastidious consumers, shopping around for the perfect product at an acceptable price.

Leaving home

Leaving a church is a serious matter. It isn't like deciding to take your money to another shop that will give you better service. Some people liken it to divorce. They argue that just as in marriage people make a public commitment to love each other, so people who join a church often make a public commitment to the rest of the membership. And certainly, if you've served in a fellowship for any reasonable length of time, the pain of leaving can be traumatic. Others have likened leaving a church to leaving the family home. Whether the departure is for positive or negative reasons, it is still a serious and stressful move.

Some ground-rules

We have developed five 'ground-rules' which we've tried to apply when we've had to consider church moves ourselves, or when we've counselled others.

1. It is never right to leave a church in order to go it alone, to try to do without church altogether.

Ruth moved to a small church in a Suffolk village from a large church in Oxford. Her former congregation was full of people who had at least one degree. It had thriving music, dance, and drama groups, an administrative support team, and an agnostics' discussion outreach. It was the kind of place where you could always find someone to argue with over the finer points of Kierkegaard, should you ever feel the need. Because she had been converted there when she was a student, Ruth half hoped that all churches would be identical to this one.

After three months of trying with Bethesda Tabernacle, she gave up and stayed at home. Although she did half-heartedly try some churches in a nearby town later, she had convinced herself that she wouldn't find what she was looking for.

Five years later she still would have called herself a Christian, although she would say, 'If you mean 'Christian' in the traditional sense, I would have to say I don't quite fit that category any more. I've grown beyond that.' Despite Ruth's real needs, she is, in effect, saying that she is superior to any local body of Christ, and she certainly will not become its servant.

When Abigail and Martin moved into a city from Bethesda Tabernacle, they too couldn't settle anywhere. You see, 'BT' had been so 'sound', and the pastor had had such a good preaching ministry. Wherever they tried, nobody quite matched up to his standards. What made matters worse was that they found that most other Christians disagreed with them over minor issues. This hadn't happened at BT.

They went to one church only to find that it had discussion-style Bible studies, and the church had replaced some hymns with new songs. Another church used a different translation of the Bible from the one their pastor had said was sound; another had a system of government that they couldn't accept; another had a basis of faith which wasn't quite Calvinistic enough for them; another ...

For the past three years they have gone nowhere. On Sundays they worship at home and listen to tapes from their former pastor. In letters to him they lament the state of the churches they have tried. Despite any real needs, they are, in effect, saying that they are superior to any local body of Christ, and they certainly will not become its servants.

A few people are so hurt by what happens to them in church, that they leave and never go to a place of worship again for years, if ever at all. At twenty-eight, Geoff was a pillar of St Michael's. He was a lay reader and a conscientious and inventive Sunday School teacher, and went to more church services and meetings than was good for his health. Everybody loved him, and people were thrilled when he met Pamela, the first and greatest love of his life (outside Christ, of course). During their two-year courtship they seemed an ideal Christian couple.

Then, three months before the wedding, Pamela ran off with the curate. Geoff stopped going to church, partly out of a misplaced sense of shame, and partly out of an equally misplaced anger at God. In his distress, he started to get drunk quite frequently. For a time he 'moved in' with a young non-Christian widow who had initially provided a shoulder to cry on, although the relationship didn't last and he soon moved out again.

Five years later, he had repented and was hungry for God. He went back to his old church, naïvely hoping that he might be welcome. A few people embraced him warmly, but others made it quite clear that he was not welcome. ('I know we're meant to forgive, but sexual sin is something different, isn't it?') So he never went again. He has never been to

123

another church since and has become very bitter about Christians. Although he may have cause to be angry, his pain has made him proud. Despite his real needs, he is, in effect, saying that he is too good for any local body of Christ, and he certainly will not become its servant.

If Christ called us to be part of a body, who are we to say that we know better?

2. It is rarely right to leave a church, without the blessing of that church, in order to set up a new church.

Yes, we know you can probably think of thriving churches that started because of an unhappy church split. But the fact that God specializes in rebuilding destroyed situations doesn't mean that we can encourage unnecessary destruction just so that we can see his grace at work.

You could have cut the atmosphere with a knife. The pastor had just announced to the church business meeting that Christopher had failed to get the majority necessary to be elected an elder. Those who had voted for him were horrified that his gifts had not been recognized by the others. The dispute, which was held beneath the surface for the next two years, erupted when John and Sophie asked if their little girl, Wendy, could be baptized by immersion.

Wendy had been dedicated in the church as a baby and had claimed conversion at three years old. Now she was ten, but John and Sophie knew that the church had a policy of not baptizing children until they were at least fifteen.

Until now John and Sophie had accepted this line uncritically, but Wendy's faith seemed so real that they couldn't understand why she should not be baptized. They had always been loyal supporters of Christopher, and they discussed it with him. He maintained that there was little (if any) biblical justification for the church's position, and a chat with some Anglican friends strengthened their feeling.

Christopher tried to take it up with the elders, but got nowhere.

This issue was the catalyst that started a major split between those who supported the existing eldership, and those who supported Christopher. And although the conversations often started with the issue of whether or not Wendy should be baptized, they soon ran on to a hundred and one other grievances that people had against those in the other camp.

During the next few months the idea of forming a new church took hold among Christopher's supporters. When faced with conflict it's always easier to run away than to stay and work to resolve it. People started to confidently say things like, 'There's no future in this church. I can't see how God can bless the present leadership . . .'

'There's a clear need for a church in that area. I'm sure God is leading us there . . .'

'God has given us Christopher to be our pastor, and if we don't take what God has clearly given to us, we'll never grow . . .'

'God has given me a clear vision for a new work . . .'

The existing eldership worked to prevent the split, but failed. They felt unable to support the 30% of the membership who left with Christopher to set up a new church. They couldn't recognize his leadership ability, and felt that the group were leaving without any real justification. Their own work was hindered by the loss of so many people, the public spectacle of an unhappy split dishonoured Christ, and reconciliation between individuals would take years (if it ever happened).

This particular church split over what was essentially a 'pastoral matter'. Often churches split over secondary matters. But whatever the particular reason, in most cases, at least two important principles are ignored.

■ The first is that, as far as we are able, we should respect and submit to the leadership that God gives us (1 Timothy 5:17–21; Hebrews 13:7, 17).

■ The second is that we should strive, as far as possible, to work to reconcile our differences with people (Colossians 3:12–14).

It may be that differences become so 'big' that everybody concerned agrees that the best way forward is for one person or party to leave. In these cases the existing leadership is trying to find a practical solution to prevent further strife. Such a move should only be a last resort after a genuine and prolonged effort has been attempted to achieve reconciliation. It should also be seen as an imperfect response to family members who feel that ideas were more important than relationships.

3. It is never right to leave a church without talking to somebody in authority in that church.

We found out almost by accident that Simon and Sonia had left the church. It was a remark they made in a phone call that made us realize they wouldn't be coming again. They had waited until the minister had left the town for a three-month sabbatical before telling anyone. They had presented him with a *fait accompli*, and to this day we don't know why. They certainly never told him and wouldn't discuss it with anyone else. Three years later they left another church in a similar manner.

Apart from being rude to the people you have committed yourself to, and who, in almost all cases, have a loving concern for you, leaving in such a manner is wrong for other reasons. We are not arguing that your reason for leaving has to be made public on all occasions, but if you have a good reason for leaving the church, you should be able to explain it to the church leaders. They may be able to point out weaknesses in what you are saying in order to help you avoid making an unhelpful mistake, or they may be able to encourage you in your decision if they agree with you.

Failure to consult the church leadership about leaving

again ignores the two principles about submission and about reconciliation of differences discussed above. If the real reason for people not talking to leaders about their leaving is because of the embarrassment of discussing differences and grievances, then leaving will not solve the problems. All that will happen is that they will be stored away to fester and be spiritually (and even physically) debilitating until they are sorted out. It is hypocrisy to want to talk to God when we won't talk to our brothers and sisters about what is on our hearts.

Christians who leave in such a way don't really appreciate that the church is a body of interrelated members, and not a clothesline of odd-shaped pegs where one can drop off if the wind gets strong.

4. It is rarely right to leave a church in a hurry.

People who leave churches in a hurry often have 'last-straw-itis' – you know, that disease which causes someone to suddenly storm out shouting, 'That's the last straw!' leaving those who remain to wonder what on earth all the fuss is about.

This disease often starts when people hold a small grudge against somebody else, or even against their church. Samantha was such a person. Perhaps Tim hadn't thanked her or consulted her in the way she thought he should. She may have misconstrued an innocent remark that wasn't intended to offend. Whatever it was, something had upset her.

And she didn't sort it out. Perhaps she didn't accept that she had a problem and tried to brush it off as insignificant. She didn't go to Tim and say, 'I have a problem with what you said/did. Please could we talk about it.'

But the problem didn't go permanently away. It hid for a while, but then kept coming back to Samantha and grew in size on each return journey. She started to discuss it with friends, and the throbbing problem grew bigger with each new conversation. And every time she went to church, this big problem grew bigger. It became like an enormous magnet that started to attract all sorts of other issues.

If Tim was late, she became disproportionately angry that he was late (although this anger was kept carefully hidden). She seemed to interpret everything he said in a negative or critical way. He was always wrong, or indirectly making remarks about her. She started to show signs of mild paranoia, convinced that Tim was out to make a fool of her, or was deliberately trying to thwart her.

This gigantic problem now ate into her prayers and her sleep. And all the time she tried to keep her anger hidden as she nursed a growing ulcer.

And finally, Tim said or did something that made her flip. 'That's it!' she thought. 'That's the straw that broke the camel's back. I'm going. I don't have to put up with this any more.' And so, in a flurry of anger, she left. On the surface she appeared to have left over something quite trivial, but the real issue was the bitterness that had been developing for months or years.

The tragedy is that Samantha need not have left at all. Much of the pain and the disruption to personal and church life could have been avoided if only she had tried to resolve the problem with Tim, or if she had stayed long enough to talk the issues through with the church leadership.

If people leave in a hurry they are usually running from something that needs to be sorted out, and are ignoring the safeguards of pastoral leadership that God has placed in churches for our own ultimate good. We place ourselves outside such safeguards to our cost. If people leave in a hurry, the chances are they haven't had time to pray the issues through, they haven't had time to examine their real motives, and they are almost certainly acting in response to their emotions, and not in response to what they and others might tell them is right in a calmer moment. Before leaving a church we need time to pray and honestly ask, 'Am I wrong?'

On rare occasions it may be necessary to leave a church in a hurry for pastoral reasons. But it should be the leaders and the people concerned who make the decision, not individuals acting in a huff.

5. It is rarely (if ever) right to leave a church because of failed relationships.

However they may choose to dress it up, it's a fact that most people leave churches over failed relationships and not over doctrine. When Christians are relating well to others in church, most would be willing to tolerate 'minor doctrinal disagreement'. It's often only when relationships break down that doctrinal differences are given greater prominence.

The surface issue was 'tongues',
> but the real issue was that I just couldn't stand the continual gossiping of one of the churchwardens. He had spread some real lies about me.

The surface issue was the form of the communion service,
> but the real issue was the lack of love and fellowship I had felt over a number of years. I got fed up with being treated like an outsider.

The surface issue was the form of church government used in this particular church,
> but the real issue was that I could no longer control the minister and get her to do exactly what I wanted.

The surface issue was infant baptism,
> but the real issue was that I wasn't asked to continue as leader of the Sunday School. I'd done the job for twenty years. How could they treat me like that?

When faced with a conflict in relationships we might deal with it in one of two ways.

■ We might *express* that conflict and 'fight'.
■ We might *suppress* that conflict and wait until it finally explodes or until we become depressed.

A few people are more naturally aggressive than others and often turn to expressing the conflict as a first option. As we noticed in chapter 6, because of a failure to appreciate that they are significant and secure in Christ, some people will always want to fight to defend their views, and will want to win at all costs.

A more common strategy for many Christians is to suppress their real feelings about something and hope that the conflict will go away. That suppression can be so extreme that people will deny that something is upsetting them, even when everybody else can see that it is. It may be that the people involved genuinely think that it is best not to say what is concerning them because they believe they should keep the peace. It may be that they are just the kind who prefer to placate others rather than risk an embarrassing and potentially painful discussion.

The strategy of suppression is as unbiblical as the strategy of expression, and is equally disastrous for individuals and churches. Although the Bible tells us to live at peace with one another as far as we are able (Romans 12:16, 18), it also condemns people who cry, 'Peace, peace,' when there is no peace (Jeremiah 6:14). We shouldn't lie that things are all right when they are not. God wants us to have harmonious relationships that are based on a true understanding of what people really think and feel, and not on a pretence. We may be very good at papering over the cracks, but God is much more interested in having them filled before we decorate. And unless we fill the cracks, they won't go away, but will rapidly grow bigger. Individuals will suffer from the physical and spiritual consequences of bitterness and churches will eventually lose members.

Unresolved anger leads to fighting or depression. Fortunately the Bible gives us an alternative strategy for dealing with conflict. God wants us to resolve conflict in a controlled way.

If a Christian has sinned against us, we are to go to the offender and explain what we think she or he has done wrong. In most cases that would lead to an apology and the end of the conflict (provided we let the matter drop and didn't keep bringing it up). If the offender feels he or she has been falsely accused, or if they won't listen to us, the matter can be established one way or the other by bringing in witnesses, or later by bringing it before the whole church (Matthew 18:15–17). And if somebody has been offended by something *we* have said or done, we are to go to them to seek reconciliation (Matthew 5:21–24).

When we go to people we should go carefully and prayerfully, struggling to produce the fruit of the Spirit. We need to be humble enough to admit that part of the problem may be our own sin, and selfless enough to want to try to reach a resolution rather than win.

The verses in Matthew state three further uncomfortable truths. The first is that *we* have to make the first move. Whether we are offended, or have caused the offence, the responsibility to go to the person concerned is ours. We have no justification for sitting back and waiting for him or her to make the first move.

The second truth is that if we refuse to be reconciled after the matter has been judged by other Christians, it is an extremely serious matter. We shouldn't go on harbouring grudges for weeks, months, years, decades, or for a lifetime, and we shouldn't put ourselves above the judgment of those whom we ask to listen to our complaint.

The third important truth is that God hates slander and unkind remarks. We should go out of our way to avoid hurting people with our words.

The writer of Proverbs says: 'As iron sharpens iron, so one man sharpens another' (Proverbs 27:17). It's immature to run away from a household just because of difficulties with relatives. We will develop good character qualities if we stay and work through problems. Similarly, if we run from church because of awkward members of our Christian family, we will miss that opportunity for growing in grace that God has planned for us, and we will only delay the day when we have to face it. We can be sure that wherever we go there will always be awkward family members with whom God wants us to learn to stay in relationship.

Leaving a church should be something that we decide to do for positive reasons, or after all else has failed. It certainly isn't something that we should choose in the heat of the moment, as a way of avoiding facing up to issues.

CHAPTER 12

REASONS FOR LEAVING A CHURCH

Is it ever right to leave a church? Yes, it clearly is on occasions. Christians will disagree as to when those occasions are. What we want to do in the remainder of this chapter is to suggest some occasions when we feel leaving may be justified. (Again, because of space limitations, we've deliberately not chosen to discuss the particular considerations that church leaders who want to leave need to take into account.)

Primary doctrinal change

In theory, it is possible for a local church or a denomination to depart from a doctrine which is part of the core of historically accepted Christian truth. For example, it may state that it no longer believes that Jesus is God. What is much more likely, however, is that an individual leader may change position on a crucial doctrine. For example, he or she may preach that individuals can find salvation through faith in people other than Jesus.

If such a thing happens, the first moves should be compassionate care and prayerful persuasion. If people stray from the truth we have a duty to gently restore them. If, however, after a period of months, no change has taken place, and if the matter has been clearly established, it would be right to try to remove the leader from a position of responsibility. If this fails, we believe it would be right to leave this particular church.

Perhaps it is more realistic not to talk of a clear-cut distinction between primary and secondary doctrine, but to imagine them at opposite ends of a continuum. In our view, the more confident we are that a doctrinal issue is secondary, the less justification we have for leaving a church. If people start to deny the physical resurrection of Jesus, we have a strong case for considering leaving. On the other hand, if we are non-charismatics and someone starts speaking in tongues, we have a great opportunity for learning to love somebody different from ourselves.

Those who argue that it is acceptable to leave over secondary doctrinal differences may end up moving churches frequently, as it is unlikely that they will be able to dot every 'i' and cross every 't' of another congregation's doctrine. The grace of Christ in our lives should enable us to love and work with those in our family who differ from us.

Honourable sending

Sometimes God may call us to serve in another place. The reassuring thing is that God is so concerned to help us avoid making mistakes, he usually uses people in our own church as part of that guidance. These are people who have known us over a period of time and can evaluate our gifts and character. God can speak to us through their collective wisdom and sensitivity to the Spirit (Acts 13:1–6).

Sometimes the 'sending' will be 'official'. There may be a special service, the laying on of hands, and perhaps financial as well as prayer support. The church is saying, 'We recognize that God is calling you to this particular work.' Although there may be visits, you may be leaving the fellowship permanently to become part of a new group of God's people.

On other occasions, the 'sending' will be a more low-key affair. After Graham became a Christian, he went to a large church on the other side of town with his friends. Several years later he began to find out more about a much smaller fellowship that worshipped just round the corner from where he lived. He began to feel a strong desire to work with the people in the smaller fellowship and help them establish an effective witness to Christ in his home area. Although he was busy serving in the large church and was very happy there, he knew that the smaller group were crying to God to send them workers. He discussed his feelings with his own church leaders, and with the pastor of the smaller fellowship. After much prayer and discussion, Graham moved to the new church. Its members were greatly encouraged. He moved with the full agreement and prayer support of his former church.

Square pegs in round holes

It's awful feeling like a square peg in a round hole, isn't it? And yet the reality is that some of us feel like that at church. Somehow we don't seem to fit any more. In the middle of a service we have this loud voice inside which keeps saying, 'This just isn't me.' It's more than just temporary dissatisfaction.

Sometimes the unease is caused by secondary doctrine.

It may be that your individual or family needs are different now from what they were ten years ago, and that your church is no longer adequately meeting them. More often, the unease is caused by differences of vision about what a church should be doing, and about how the church should go about doing it. Perhaps new people in the church have changed it beyond recognition. Perhaps you feel that God has been doing a deep work in you that has made you yearn to reform existing practices, or to start something new in the church.

Although the change may have been introduced by others, you will have to be gracious enough to accept that part of the problem is with you. Probably you can see that there is nothing wrong with what they have done. You just don't like change. God, however, may want to teach you things through these changes and through your own discomfort. We suggest you stay for as long as you can and try to come to terms with what has happened. God may want to knock some corners off you.

If you feel unease because you are yearning to bring change to your church, we also suggest that you stay in your church for as long as you are able. There are two reasons for this. The first is that your own thinking and feelings may be wrong and may need to be tested over time through prayer and discussion with people who know you and love you. The second is that God may wish to use you to bring about the changes in the church, and they are not likely to happen in the immediate future unless you stay.

We are realistic enough, however, to accept that sometimes neither the peg nor the hole is going to change in the short term. The unease by the lack of fit can quickly grow into real distress and become increasingly harmful unless it is dealt with. Sometimes, if differences become too great to live with, it would be best to find another part of God's varied family. This is different from 'shopping around' because the people involved have spent some time considering the matter carefully; they have discussed it with the church leadership, resolved any conflicts in relationships as far as they are able, and fully intend to be committed to a new church.

A career move

Many people change churches in order to take up a new job in a different part of the country. God wants Christians to serve him by being salt and light at every level in a wide range of jobs and professions. And if this is to take place, Christians will have to move.

We want to suggest, however, that instead of making a career-move decision and *then* thinking about the consequences for the church, the consequences for the church should be taken into account *when coming to a decision*. It is not right, on every occasion, to leave a church in order to take up promotion.

If someone is clearly being used by God in a particular place, he or she should think very carefully before moving. A decision to move means becoming more preoccupied than usual with the cares of this life for at least two years. During this time key Christian workers will be primarily concerned with the hassle of selling and buying houses, with settling into a new home, a new area, a new job, and a new church, and with settling children into new schools. Clearly some moves can be justified, but that justification shouldn't be seen as a foregone conclusion in every case. The work of a few churches is seriously hindered because of the high turnover of its members, some of whom may be serving their careers at the expense of Christ.

We know of people who have taken early retirement or have asked for a demotion so that they would have more free time available to serve their local churches. We know of others who have so strongly believed that they couldn't leave the work which God had called them to, that they put their career on a 'back burner' until they felt free to move. Facing church family responsibilities often involves sacrifice.

Seeing the beauty

Have you ever tried to capture the beauty of a sunset on film? When the prints come back, people can respond in very different ways. Some may be disappointed, complaining about camera wobble, poor colour saturation, or noticeable grain on the film. They might moan about the composition and wish that a tree or a river could have been moved a few inches to the right. But others stand in silence for a few seconds. The subtle hues and shadows, the majestic expanse of sky, momentarily fill them with a sense of awe. The first group want to throw the photograph away. It doesn't meet their standards. The second group want to keep it and will passionately defend it against all detractors. For them, its beauty is greater than its minor imperfections.

Perhaps for too long we have become preoccupied with the failures of our local congregation. We need to regain a sense of wonder at what God is building. The church is far from perfect, but its splendour is far greater than Satan would have us believe. This is because Jesus is building it. In our last two chapters we consider the part we have to play in extending his kingdom.

CHAPTER 13

HOPE IN A HOPELESS CHURCH

Jesus goes to church

If you look at the state of the Christian church in your town, city, or village, what do you see?

On occasions we can paint a depressing picture. Our vision can be dominated by scenes of members of the Christian family hurting each other with words so searing that they blister the heart. There may be rebellion, disunity, and a failure to take seriously the tasks of evangelism, discipleship training, and social care. On the other hand, if sometimes we see the church through mud-spattered spectacles, at other times we view it through syrup. There is nothing wrong with our 'little place of worship', and woe to the person who dares to suggest that there might be! It's sweet being there, and we are addicted to, and deceived by, the taste.

In our more realistic moments we know the church to be both good and bad. Yes, there is pain and frustration, anger, and weeping. There *are* many things that need to be done. But there is also so much that is good, because Jesus dwells with and works through his people.

We see the love of Christ in the regular visits to the housebound lady, and in the meals provided for the new widower and his children. It's there in the compassionate care that is given to the young homeless.

In times of worship, we catch glimpses of the joy of Christ, when the words of a song suddenly hit home in a fresh way. It's there too in fellowship, when we are so glad of the other family members. The peace of Christ peeps out when the rebellious daughter finishes her confession and knows that she is loved and forgiven by God, or when a father finally accepts that God is in control, even of his unemployment and of his children's health.

The patience of Christ shines through the wife regularly praying for her husband to be converted, through the counsellor persevering with the schizophrenic, and through the rector who is struggling to cope with a PCC member who is stuck in his ways. Patience is also there, together with the faithfulness of Christ, in the evangelist who goes on sowing in the dusty earth, always looking for the harvest to come.

The Sunday School teacher who every week graciously brings sweets and learning to a class of eight-year-old boys demonstrates the kindness, goodness, gentleness and self-control of Christ. These qualities shine in the elder who is asked to stand down after thirty years of solid service, and who remains as committed to the church as ever. And you can see them in the family who take a physically handicapped teenager on holiday so that a single parent can have a break. They are there too in the minister who quietly continues to craft the next sermon, despite the accusing phone call that had made his wife cry.

We shouldn't be blind to Jesus who is present in his church. In the remainder of this chapter we want to examine some more biblical reasons for hope by looking at the situation in one church in some detail.

Case study: Finding hope

How would you begin a letter to a church that appeared to be in a very bad state? That was the problem facing one pastor when he was away on a missionary journey, prevented from addressing in person the problems that people had reported to him.

The year was about AD 54.[1] Although he had had months of effective ministry in the city (Acts 18), the mice had started to play when the cat had gone away. Paul had to write to a church where some rejected his teaching and were fighting each other. It was full of cliques, each following a different personality. The rich kept themselves to themselves and the poor were left alone. There was little church discipline, and a distinct lack of humility and of concern for others. In morals, the church was being influenced *by* the city rather than setting the standard *for* it.

Corinth itself was an extremely unlikely place for a church to grow strong. It was an important port that was also notorious as a centre of immorality. The Greeks had a word, 'to Corinthianize', which meant 'to live in drunken and immoral debauchery'. There was little hope in the city, and little hope in the church. So, how would you begin a letter to a group of Christians who were causing you much concern?

God is the perfect personnel manager

Paul begins 1 Corinthians with the key word 'called' (1:1, 2, 9). In one sense, he is challenging his critics. He is reminding those who questioned his apostolic ministry that they are answerable to God, because God called him to do a job. If they reject him they are rejecting God. But then he reminds them that they too have been called. If there is hope for the

141

Corinthian church, part of it lies in the fact that God is its perfect personnel manager.

It's as if Paul was saying: 'You may be having problems with me, and I'm certainly having problems with you, but we can be hopeful because God knows what he is doing. He has chosen us to be together. It *isn't* some awful mistake! We may want to close the church down and start again with a new set of people of our own choice. But that is looking at it from a human point of view. Knowing everything about our sinful past and our potential for the future, God has chosen *us*. He has called us to be holy, to be part of a called-out people. And he has called us into fellowship with others who share this calling. We're not perfect, but we are "picked"; we're not superstars, but we are "selected". There's no going it alone, and no rejecting others.'

When God brings people into the church, we may want to challenge the 'appointments' he has made. But let's remember that the perfect personnel manager had access to information that was unavailable to us. God is calling people to be together and to be in Christ. Jesus is building his church with hand-picked people. Peter's impetuosity might be the first thing to strike us, but Christ saw beyond this to his steadfastness and the rock that he was going to become. We see somebody's temper, or their frustrating inability to organize. But Christ sees their generosity or doctrinal maturity which are needed in a particular congregation.

God is the greatest giver

In 1 Corinthians 1:4–7, Paul made three statements about the lavish generosity of God towards the Corinthians. He told them:

■ His grace was given you.

■ In every way you were enriched.

■ You are not lacking in any spiritual gift.

Sometimes it's easy for us to despair about our

142

churches and to focus on what we haven't got. 'We haven't got any maturity,' or, 'We haven't got any young people.' 'We haven't got any accountants or talented musicians.' 'We haven't got any real love.' 'Our worship is terrible.' 'We haven't got ...' 'We're hopeless.' But to a church which didn't have perfection or unity Paul wrote to remind them that in Christ they were rich. The word translated 'enriched' (verse 5) gives us our English word 'plutocrat' – a very rich person. Despite their great problems, they were spiritually very well endowed.

In case the Corinthians thought they were hard done by, Paul reminded them of the grace that had been given to them as a body. He told them that they had spiritual powers of both speech (*logos*) and knowledge (*gnōsis*). On the 'speech' side they had gifts of teaching, evangelism, prophecy, tongues, and interpretation of tongues. As far as knowledge was concerned, Paul reminded them that, as a body of Christians, they had access to the secrets of the universe and could draw upon wisdom, discernment, and insight through the Holy Spirit.

And the richness that the Corinthian church had in Christ was more than a cold statement of theological fact. It was a living reality. Paul had seen it and could write: '... our testimony about Christ was confirmed in you' (verse 6). Despite all the problems in the church, there was hope because he could see the Holy Spirit working in their lives. Even if the evidence seems very thin at times, wherever there are Christians, there *is* evidence of the Spirit working.

Imagine a mid-week prayer meeting of this Corinthian congregation. They may have sat and looked miserable, very conscious of who wasn't there, harbouring ill feelings to some of those who were present, depressed by their present plight. Into this situation of immorality, division, and doctrinal confusion, Paul wants to bring hope. 'Look,' he says, 'you can't deny the reality of what you have experienced.

143

God is doing something in you. In the middle of this chaos and pain there is spiritual life. Don't just focus on what you haven't got, but on what you do have in Christ. And what you have in Christ is worth far more than anything the world can offer. There is hope because of what God is able to provide for you and to do in you. You're not bankrupt. The Holy Spirit has brought you to life. The Holy Spirit wants to bring you to perfection.'

God is the most capable keeper

Paul is positive about the origins of the church and about its present resources. He is also positive about the church's ultimate future because it is going to be completely sustained by the faithfulness of God.

If you're struggling to cope with your church, prepare to be excited! *'He will keep you strong to the end, so that you will be blameless on the day of our Lord Jesus Christ'* (1 Corinthians 1:8).

To an apparently hopeless and extremely difficult congregation, Paul says: 'Look at your spiritual foundations, at your present spiritual resources. And look at your future spiritual destiny and who it is who guarantees your arrival.'

The only thing that enables us to cope with the church is not the people, but God's ability to forgive us and empower us to behave like his children. Paul is sure of the faithfulness of God. He who called them into fellowship with his Son, Jesus Christ our Lord, is faithful. If you are tempted to doubt that hope for the church lies in God's wisdom and power and not in people, take a toddler and walk with him across a busy road. The security of the child lies in the strength and judgment of the more capable adult, not in those of the child.

The writer of Numbers recorded a prophecy that described God's character: 'God is not a man, that he should lie, nor a son of man, that he should change his mind. Does he speak and then not act? Does he promise and not fulfil?' (Numbers 23:19). Because God promises to sustain the church, we can be confident that he will supply the spiritual (and material) resources to help us through the toughest times.

When we feel intense pressure to give up because of our unique church situation, Paul reminds us: 'No temptation has seized you except what is common to man. And God is faithful; he will not let you be tempted beyond what you can bear. But when you are tempted, he will also provide a way out so that you can stand up under it' (1 Corinthians 10:13).

And when situations are so painful that we cannot understand why God allows them to continue, when we feel at the end of our tether physically, spiritually, emotionally and intellectually, when we know that we cannot stand any more, Paul reminds us of a time when God said to him: 'My grace is sufficient for you, for my power is made perfect in weakness' (2 Corinthians 12:9). We worship a living, enabling, compassionate God, not a lump of stone.

The fact that God will keep his church doesn't mean that it is going to be easy for individuals, or that congregations are going to be trouble-free. In the short term, individual fellowships may have to close. The congregation in Corinth needed to take a hard look at itself. Where there is disobedience, God doesn't want to hide it, but wants us to turn from it. Some Christians in Corinth were going to have to weep as they faced up to sin. Some were going to be angry and insulted by what God said about them. But in the long term, Paul knew that God was going to keep them. He is building his church, and the gates of hell will not prevail against it.

And in spite of present, local difficulties, there will be a day when Jesus will present his perfect bride. God will ensure that no charge or accusation is levelled against his people. On that day it will be clear to all that not only did he call us, but that he also justified us and kept us; not only did he justify and keep us, but he also glorified us. One day we will be part of the perfect church that Jesus has built.

It's God's church, not ours. Its resources are not just human, but divine as well. When all that we can see about a congregation is the mess, we need to keep a biblical perspective before us. He can cope with it, and he can give us the grace to cope as well. God is so passionately committed to his church, he sent his Son to die for it. Jesus has defeated the raging lion that wants to devour the flock. Therefore it *is* possible for Christians to overcome the evil within the church as well as the evil outside it. Jesus hasn't abandoned the church, and neither should we.

14

KINGDOM WORKERS

Have you ever made a new friend and then realized that the reality of the person's character and beliefs was different from what you had initially assumed? The disciples of Jesus must have had as great a shock as they tried to grapple with the fact that what Jesus was teaching them about his kingdom was so different from what they were anticipating.

Many Jews were looking for the establishment of a new kingdom, and the disciples were no exception. Since the return from the Babylonian exile, this proud people had been ruled by the Greeks and then by the Romans. They naturally interpreted the prophecies about a king setting up a kingdom in a literal way. They wanted a Jesus who would fight like Joshua. They wanted a Son of David who would fight like David. They wanted a Messiah who would set up an earthly kingdom. We are told in John 6:15 that a group of them wanted to make Jesus king. James and John argued about post-conquest sharing of power (Mark 10:35–39). Even after the resurrection, some of the disciples were still asking questions about an earthly kingdom (Acts 1:6).

Jesus had to slowly teach people that his kingdom would be different. Christ's reign would not be a cataclysmic, external triumph of an earthly Messiah, but a 'quiet', revolutionary rule over hearts (Luke 17:21). His kingdom would not be in a place, but in people. It would be established not by military subjugation, but by personal submission to the rule of God. The evidence of the kingdom would not be the destruction of an earthly power such as Rome, but the overthrow of spiritual domination by Satan in the lives of individuals.

Read through the exciting opening chapter of Mark's gospel and watch the kingdom of God growing before your eyes. After calling his fellow kingdom workers, Jesus goes to Capernaum and immediately there is conflict with Satan. The influence of evil is challenged and defeated as demons are rebuked and people healed. When Peter declares that Jesus is the Christ (Mark 8:29), we see the kingdom light slowly dispelling the spiritual darkness of the disciples' understanding.

But note that the kingdom is *not* the church. The kingdom is the rule of God in the lives of individuals. The church is a group of people in whom the kingdom is growing, but the church is not the kingdom itself. When we pray, 'Your kingdom come, your will be done on earth as it is in heaven,' we shouldn't just be thinking of God answering that request by making the church grow numerically or by defeating evil in society. We should also be longing that God's rule will be extended in the lives of individuals *within* the church. We should be praying that Christians will be able to overcome the evil that is brought into the church, in their own lives, and in the lives of others.

If we are to cope with church life, we don't just need a biblically based hope, but also the kingdom character – those qualities that God wants to build in the kingdom workers. Jesus begins the Sermon on the Mount by giving us a positive picture of what the kingdom workers should be like (Matthew 5:3–12). John Stott has argued[1] that the Beatitudes can be taken to describe a single group of people and not eight separate groups – people who are at the same time meek and merciful, poor in spirit and pure in heart, mourning and hungry, peacemakers and persecuted.

Blessed are the poor in spirit

Jesus commends those who are poor in spirit (Matthew 5:3), not those who are spiritually arrogant. The kingdom doesn't belong to those who think they deserve it and who are complacent about their own spiritual state, but to those who are conscious of their own sin. 'This is the one I esteem,' says God. Who? The one who shouts the loudest and wins all the battles in church meetings? The one who is always quick to tell others that they are wrong? The one who is always boasting about what he has done? No! 'He who is humble and contrite in spirit, and trembles at my word' (Isaiah 66:2).

We won't be able to cope with church as long as we set ourselves up over others and condemn them. However much other Christians annoy and frustrate us, we need to look first to the planks in our own eyes before seeking to remove the specks from those of others (Matthew 7:1–5). Tut-tutting over someone else's lack of vision may boost our ego, but it doesn't address the issue of our pride. When we are more honest about our own sin, we will become more sympathetic to the temptations faced by others, and more dependent on God for grace.

Blessed are those who mourn

We don't normally think of people in mourning as being blessed. In the context, however, Jesus is not promising the spiritual benefits of the kingdom to everyone who is bereaved (clearly not everyone will enter the kingdom of heaven), but to those who experience deep sorrow because of sin (Matthew 5:4). And this sorrow is so intense that people are likely to want to do something about it. It's one thing to acknowledge that we need to change our character. It's another thing to grieve so much over its sinful effects in our own life, and over its influence on others, that we make moves to repent.

If we are to cope with church life, we need to learn to move away from attacking the sinners and towards sharing something of God's grief over the sin. We need to move from bitterness about individuals towards passionate concern about what is happening in their lives and in the life of the church.

The psalmist wrote: 'Streams of tears flow from my eyes, for your law is not obeyed' (Psalm 119:136). When describing the effects of sin in the lives of some, Paul wrote: 'For, as I have often told you before and now say again even with tears, many live as enemies of the cross of Christ' (Philippians 3:18). As we try to cope with the church, our prayer should be:

> *Soften my heart, Lord, soften my heart.*
> *From all indifference set me apart.*
> *To feel your compassion, to weep with your tears,*
> *Soften my heart, O Lord, soften my heart.*

Blessed are the meek

There seem to be at least two ideas behind the word translated 'meek'. It was used in connection with stallions who had been broken in. The word had associations of power under control. It is also connected with the soothing qualities of ointment. Perhaps meekness is best described as

150

self-control and kindness. We clearly see the meekness of Christ in his response to his enemies. Sometimes he is silent. Often his answers pierce through to the heart of the matter in order to help people face the truth. Jesus is no doormat, but neither is he a bully, or a bull in a china shop.

Meekness is essential for coping with church life. Without it, we sin in anger. We become rough and overbearing in order to get our own way. As we saw in chapter 6, we need to learn to rest in Christ, confident that our significance and security are in him. When we are at peace in the status he gives us, we can have the strength to control our powerful words, to curb our destructive looks, and to initiate actions of love to those who thwart us.

Blessed are those who hunger and thirst for righteousness

Although we all have many desires, only three of them must be satisfied for basic living – air, food, water. Jesus takes two of these primary desires and uses them to describe the characteristic longing that the kingdom workers are to cultivate and seek to satisfy (Matthew 5:6).

The picture is one of people who are constantly coming to God for food, pleading for life-giving nourishment. These are not proud people who can stay at a distance and feel self-satisfied about what they have, or about what is happening. They know that they will grow weak and perish unless they stay close to God. Hungry to do his will, they strive for righteousness in their personal lives, in the life of the church, and in the life of society. They don't expect to extend God's kingdom by moaning and by keeping him at arm's length. They know they will have to struggle, and they know they need spiritual resources.

Blessed are the merciful

Being merciful (Matthew 5:7) means caring for those in misery and having a forgiving spirit. Perhaps it's the latter meaning which has most relevance in this context. Coping with church life means forgiving others.

Forgiveness is very difficult if we are proud, complacent, impetuous, and indifferent about obedience. It is certainly easier if we cultivate humility, self-control, kindness, and a passionate desire to do what God wants.

Often we want to put boundaries on forgiveness. The two most obvious ways we try to limit it concern the sins we are willing to cover, and the number of times we are to forgive. We might be willing to forgive someone who carelessly failed to make a promised visit to a hospital, but unwilling to forgive her if she had an affair with the organist. But God places no such limits on what can be forgiven. We may be willing to forgive a person once, but not if he continues to fall in the same sin. Again, God places no limits on the number of times we are to forgive (Luke 17:3).

Dave and Joyce Ames point out that forgiveness is not a feeling but an act of the will.[2] We can choose to forgive, or not to forgive. Failure to do so in homes leads to stress and causes the breakup of families. And similar things happen in churches unless we decide to move beyond being sorry about our own sin before God to reach out to others in forgiveness of their sin. Because of the problems caused by spiritual failure, we will not be able to cope with church life unless we learn to forgive others all their sins on every occasion. The best way to learn is to start practising.

Blessed are the pure in heart

Dr Lawrence Crabb has argued[3] that many Christians don't really develop enough spiritually, despite many years in the faith. This is because we sometimes think righteousness is just about going to church, and about not swearing and not getting drunk. We tend to ignore the inner dimension of growing in love for God, and of conquering sinful attitudes that aren't always immediately apparent in our external behaviour.

Jesus wants kingdom workers to have an inward purity (Matthew 5:8). He wants us to have the kind of righteousness that grieves over gossip at home and silences it there, as well as one which publicly condemns it at church. He wants the holiness of character that privately yearns for God and prays for his kingdom to come in the silences of the night, as well as in the glare of the prayer meeting. He wants forgiveness which stays forgiveness, and patience which stays patience, once a person's back is turned and she or he is out of earshot. Until we are determined to strive for this kind of righteousness and accept nothing less, we will be helping Satan in his attempt to destroy the church.

Blessed are the peacemakers

Peacemaking (Matthew 5:9) doesn't mean 'trying to lead a quiet life at all costs'. Sometimes we will have to disturb things in the short term in order to bring a lasting peace. If relationships are wrong they have to be put right so that they don't fester for years and then explode. And putting them right may involve unavoidable conflict in the short term.

Peacemakers know that peace in the church doesn't just happen, and for the most part, it isn't some mysterious cloud that God drops. They know that if evil is to be defeated in church life, peace has to be worked for. Peacemaking involves courage and can be costly (as Jesus knows). You have to take the initiative and compassionately talk about issues which people may well wish to keep hidden. You risk failure and could end up being misunderstood. But peacemakers see their work as a positive strategy for coping with church life and for extending God's kingdom. They are a 'chip off the old block', sharing their master's work of reconciliation (Colossians 1:20).

Blessed are those who are persecuted because of righteousness

We have argued that the church is not the kingdom. As we try to extend God's kingdom in the church, we may well face serious opposition from other Christians who are being used by Satan to resist the extension of that kingdom. And we too may be guilty of resisting the kingdom-building that is being done by others.

Effective preachers may be rejected as they bring God's truth to people and disturb 'safe' thought patterns. Satan wants people to keep believing unbiblical ideas. Passionate evangelists may be resisted because their example and schemes challenge complacency. Satan prefers people not to hear the gospel. Skilful administrators may encounter a hostile reception for their suggestions because Satan likes to maintain a state of ineffective chaos. Able counsellors may have to struggle to have their proposals for a plan of action taken seriously by the church because Satan doesn't want the wounded to be bound up or the tired lambs to be carried. In whatever way you work to build God's kingdom, there will be opposition; and as you work in the church, most of that opposition will come from other Christians.

Although we should not go looking for persecution, it may help us to cope if we know that we will be persecuted by others in the church. As we become more like the King, we are not so easily surprised by the opposition, and we learn to accept it as inevitable in this life. (But, just in case we are tempted to take the attitude which says, 'I'm being opposed, therefore I must be right,' being poor in spirit should remind us to have a healthy degree of self-doubt.)

The Beatitudes describe eight different characteristics of the kingdom workers. They are the blueprint for how to respond to church life successfully. None of us yet has all those qualities to the extent that God wants. His kingdom is still growing in us. In case we should feel that they represent an unattainable goal for us, however, we need to remember that Jesus is on our side, working in co-operation with us, to build those things in our lives. The alternative to each one of them is evil and destructive. As we work to overcome pride, gloating over sin, lack of self-control, unkindness, an indifference to God and his will, an unwillingness to forgive, hypocrisy, an unwillingness to create a meaningful peace, and an avoidance of doing what is right for fear of persecution, we can take heart. 'The reason the Son of God appeared was to destroy the devil's work' (1 John 3:8).

Saying words and knowing truth aren't enough

Coping with church life is not about changing others, but about changing ourselves. We sometimes talk about not being able to cope, and we tend to blame fellow Christians. But God empowers us to cope with his church as we work to develop the character that he wants us to have.

At the end of the Sermon on the Mount Jesus challenges us to look at the excuses that we give for not obeying him (Matthew 7:21–27). As John Stott has noted,[4] Jesus places spiritual responsibility on those who listen and read as well as on those who speak and write. How well have we heard the message of this book?

If we want to cope with church life we will have to

move beyond saying sound words. 'Not everyone who says to me "Lord, Lord," will enter the kingdom of heaven, but only he who does the will of my Father who is in heaven' (Matthew 7:21). The acid test of true spirituality and love for God is obedience. Making statements to God such as, 'I believe being committed to a church is a good thing,' or 'I believe forgiving others is the way to cope with difficult relationships,' doesn't cut any ice. God wants us to make that difficult journey, to say those difficult words, and to do those difficult deeds. According to Christ, we are idiots if we hear but do not obey (Matthew 7:26–27).

Many of us find it relatively easy to keep up an appearance of religious orthodoxy, and to make the right noises to visitors about our churches and the people in them. We know how to keep the inward evil hidden. But Christianity is about on-going repentance, and coping with church life is about turning from evil, not adding to it or covering it up. God requires not just a verbal pretence, but a conscious striving to turn bitterness into love, selfishness into sacrifice, impatience into longsuffering, and anger into peace.

If we choose not to cope with church, we are people who like the trappings of religion without the radical claims. We might as well put the following advert in the personal column of the local newspaper: 'Fun-loving person seeks divinity for mutual diversion on Sundays. No ties or commitment.'[5]

The question Jesus asks is not, '*Can* you cope with church life?' (he already knows the answer to that), but '*Will* you cope with it for me?' And as we reflect on that second question, let's remember that 'the eyes of the LORD range throughout the earth, to strengthen those who are committed to him' (2 Chronicles 16:9). May God look on us and strengthen us in our desire to be his disciples.

156

NOTES

Chapter 2

1 See *The New Bible Dictionary* (IVP, 2nd edn., 1982): the entry 'Church' gives a full discussion of this point.
2 Jesus rarely talked about 'the church' (Matthew 18:17 is the one recorded instance), but he often described the kingdom of God (and the kingdom of heaven). Although, as we shall argue in a later chapter, the kingdom of God is not the same as the church, there is considerable overlap, because Christians are part of the kingdom.
3 See also John 15:26–27; 16:12–15; compare 1 Corinthians 2:9–13.
4 See, for example, Mark 1:35; Luke 6:12; John 17:1–26.
5 See, for example, Matthew 6:5–14; Luke 11:1–12.
6 See *The New Bible Dictionary* entry 'Communion' for a discussion on 'fellowship' in the New Testament.
7 See also 1 Corinthians 1:9; Philippians 2:1; 1 Peter 5:1.

Chapter 3

1 For an excellent book on the subject see Derek Wood's *The Barnabas Factor* (IVP, 1988).

Chapter 4

1 John Stott and David L. Edwards, *Essentials* (Hodder and Stoughton, 1988), pp. 105–106.

Chapter 5

1 The story is told by David Bridge and Donald Phypers in *The Water that Divides* (IVP, 1977), p. 95.
2 Murray Watts, *Rolling in the Aisles* (Marc, 1987), p. 92.
3 Although the NIV translates Romans 16:7 as speaking of another male apostle, Junias, there are strong linguistic reasons for arguing that the term refers to a female. See Leon Morris, *The Epistle to the Romans* (Eerdmans/IVP, 1988). Early commentators thought the verse referred to a married couple.
4 Michael Green, *To Corinth with Love* (Hodder and Stoughton, 1982), p. 159.

Chapter 6

1 Lawrence Crabb, *Effective Biblical Counselling* (Marshalls, 1985), p. 57.
2 See also Matthew 7:15; Philippians 1:10; 1 Corinthians 5; 1 Timothy 1:6–7; Titus 3:10.
3 Joyce Huggett, *Conflict: Friend or Foe?* (Kingsway, 1984).
4 Stephen Gaukroger and Nick Mercer, *Frogs in Cream* (Scripture Union, 1990), p. 105.
5 Murray Watts, *Rolling in the Aisles*, p. 27.

Chapter 8

1 Donald Bridge, *How to Spot a Church Split and Do Something About It* (Marc, 1989), p. 26.

Chapter 10

1 Several Bible colleges offer correspondence courses. For example, London Bible College, Green Lane, Northwood, Middlesex, HA6 2UW, offers a range of short courses.

2 Especially those written by people who have experienced heartache and suffering, such as the many books written by Joni Eareckson Tada, or David Watson's account of the last year of his life (*Fear No Evil*, Hodder and Stoughton, 1984).

3 By Elleston Trevor.

4 Dave Ames. See Dave and Joyce Ames, *Looking Up the Aisle?* (Kingsway, 1989).

Chapter 13

1 The material in this case study has been based on David Prior's exposition of 1 Corinthians 1:1–10 in *The Message of 1 Corinthians* (IVP, 1985).

Chapter 14

1 John Stott, *The Message of the Sermon on the Mount* (IVP, 1978), p. 31.

2 Dave and Joyce Ames, *Stress-Free Marriage* (Crossway, 1990), chapter 6.

3 Lawrence Crabb, *Inside Out* (Navpress, 1980).

4 John Stott, *The Message of the Sermon on the Mount*, pp. 206ff.

5 Adapted from Mike Starkey, *Born To Shop* (Monarch, 1989), p. 226.